EDITOR: Maryanne Blacker

FOOD EDITOR: Pamela Clark

■ ■ ■

ART DIRECTOR: Verna McGeachin

ARTIST: Annemarlene Hissink

■ ■ ■

ASSISTANT FOOD EDITOR: Louise Patniotis

ASSOCIATE FOOD EDITOR: Enid Morrison

SENIOR HOME ECONOMISTS:
Kathy McGarry, Sophia Young

HOME ECONOMISTS: Angela Bresnahan, Janene Brooks,
Justin Kerr, Caroline Merrillees, Maria Sampsonis, Jodie Tilse,
Amal Webster, Lovoni Welch

EDITORIAL COORDINATOR: Elizabeth Hooper

KITCHEN ASSISTANT: Amy Wong

■ ■ ■

STYLISTS: Marie-Helene Clauzon, Carolyn Fienberg,
Jane Hann, Jacqui Hing, Cherise Koch

PHOTOGRAPHERS: Robert Clark, Robert Taylor

■ ■ ■

HOME LIBRARY STAFF:

ART DIRECTOR: Sue de Guingand

ASSISTANT EDITORS: Bridget Green, Lynne Testoni

EDITORIAL COORDINATOR: Fiona Lambrou

■ ■ ■

ACP PUBLISHER: Richard Walsh

ACP DEPUTY PUBLISHER: Nick Chan

ACP CIRCULATION & MARKETING DIRECTOR:
Judy Kiernan

■ ■ ■

Produced by The Australian Women's Weekly Home Library.
Cover separations by ACP Colour Graphics Pty Ltd., Sydney.
Colour separations by Network Graphics Pty. Ltd., Sydney.
Printing by Hannanprint, Sydney.
Published by ACP Publishing Pty. Limited,
54 Park Street, Sydney.
◆ AUSTRALIA: Distributed by Network Distribution
Company, 54 Park Street, Sydney, (02) 282 8777.
◆ UNITED KINGDOM: Distributed in the U.K. by Australian
Consolidated Press (UK) Ltd, 20 Galowhill Rd, Brackmills,
Northampton NN4 7EE (01604) 760 456.
◆ CANADA: Distributed in Canada by Whitecap Books Ltd,
351 Lynn Ave, North Vancouver B.C. V7J 2C4 (604) 980 9852.
◆ NEW ZEALAND: Distributed in New Zealand by Netlink
Distribution Company, 17B Hargreaves St, Level 5,
College Hill, Auckland 1 (9) 302 7616.
◆ SOUTH AFRICA: Distributed in South Africa by Intermag,
PO Box 57394, Springfield 2137 (011) 493 3200.

■ ■ ■

Middle Eastern Easy Style Cookery

Includes index.
ISBN 1 86396 034 1

1. Cookery, Middle Eastern. I. Title:
Australian Women's Weekly. (Series:
Australian Women's Weekly Home Library).

641.5956

■ ■ ■

© A C P Publishing Pty. Limited 1996
ACN 053 273 546
◆ This publication is copyright. No part of it may be
reproduced or transmitted in any form without the written
permission of the publishers.

■ ■ ■

COVER: Clockwise from back: Tahini Dip, page 2;
Tabbouleh, page 58; Almond Coriander Couscous, page 73;
Chicken Tagine with Dates and Honey, page 23;
Lavash, page 77.
Ceramic lamp, tiles and plate from Country Floors;
tagine dish and bowls from Francalia; silver servers from
Accoutrement; rug from Mr Brassman.
OPPOSITE: Layered Eggplant and Pepper Salad, page 70.
BACK COVER: Figs in Honey and Port Wine, page 96.

MIDDLE EASTERN

Eas... ...kery

Whether in Mo... ...rkey, Egypt, Tunisia or
anywhere in and around the Middle East, you discover an
intense love of cooking, eating and hospitality. A great many
dishes are common to each country; traditions intermingle and
the cultures are similar, so the food itself, while distinctively
delicious, can be considered one fascinating and inspirational
cuisine. We give you a superb cross-section, easily translating
recipes from the Middle East to your own table.

Pamela Clark

FOOD EDITOR

Australian Catalogue Co.
7412 Wingfoot Dr.
Raleigh, NC 27615
919-878-8266

BRITISH & NORTH AMERICAN READERS: Please note that
Australian cup and spoon measurements are metric. A quick
conversion guide appears on page 127.
A glossary explaining unfamiliar terms and ingredients
appears on page 124.

Snacks & Starters

Dip into some delicious starters. Try your hand at Lebanese favourites such as baba ghanoush or hummus, or enjoy the spicy lamb pizzas and mixed vegetable pickles. Exotic dips appear with bread at every table throughout the Middle East, and many dishes featured here also double as scrumptious snacks.

Tahini Dip

12 cloves garlic
2 teaspoons ground cumin
1 teaspoon grated lemon rind
2/3 cup (160ml) tahini
1/2 cup (125ml) lemon juice
1/2 cup (125ml) water

3. Add combined juice and water gradually in a thin stream while motor is operating, process until combined. Spoon into serving bowl, sprinkle with a little extra ground cumin, serve with toasted pita bread, if desired.
Makes about 1 1/2 cups (375ml).

■ Recipe can be made 2 days ahead.
■ Storage: Covered, in refrigerator.
■ Freeze: Not suitable.
■ Microwave: Not suitable.

1. Place unpeeled garlic cloves on oven tray, bake, uncovered, in hot oven about 10 minutes or until garlic is soft; cool. Remove skin from cloves.

2. Blend or process garlic, cumin, rind and tahini until combined.

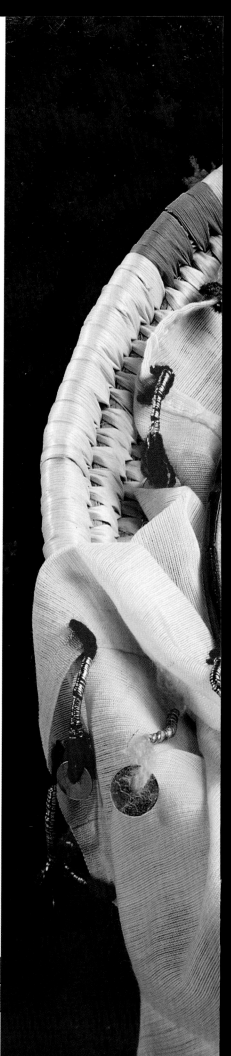

Basket from The Bay Tree Kitchen Shop.

Broad Bean Dip

1/3 cup (80ml) olive oil
1 medium (150g) onion,
　　finely chopped
1 clove garlic, crushed
1 teaspoon ground cumin
pinch cayenne pepper
500g frozen broad beans,
　　thawed, peeled
3/4 cup (180ml) water
1 tablespoon lemon juice
1 tablespoon chopped fresh dill

1. Heat 1 tablespoon of the oil in pan, add onion, garlic, cumin and pepper, cook, stirring, until onion is soft. Add beans, cook, stirring, 5 minutes.

2. Blend or process bean mixture, remaining oil, water and lemon juice until well combined.

3. Return bean mixture to same pan, stir over heat until heated through; stir in dill. Sprinkle warm dip with a little extra cayenne pepper, if desired. Serve with vegetable sticks.
Makes about 2 cups (500ml).

■ Recipe can be made a day ahead.
■ Storage: Covered, in refrigerator.
■ Freeze: Not suitable.
■ Microwave: Suitable.

Serving bowls from The Bay Tree Kitchen Shop.

Plates from Orson & Blake Collectables; fabric from Joan Bowers Antiques.

Stuffed Mussels

You will need to cook ⅓ cup (65g)
long-grain rice for this recipe.

18 (900g) green-lipped mussels
½ cup (125ml) dry white wine
2 teaspoons olive oil
3 green shallots, chopped
1 cup cooked white rice
⅓ cup (35g) toasted
**   pistachios, chopped**
1 tablespoon dried currants
1 tablespoon chopped fresh parsley
1 tablespoon chopped fresh
**   coriander leaves**
2 teaspoons chopped fresh mint
1 teaspoon grated lemon rind
2 teaspoons honey
60g butter, melted
1½ tablespoons lemon juice

2. Add wine and mussels to large pan, simmer, covered, over medium heat about 2 minutes or until mussels open. Drain mussels; discard liquid and any unopened mussels.

4. Discard half of each shell. Place mussels in their remaining half shells on oven trays, drizzle with combined juice and remaining butter. Fill with rice mixture. Bake, uncovered, in hot oven about 5 minutes or until hot.
Makes 18.

■ Recipe can be prepared
   3 hours ahead.
■ Storage: Covered, in refrigerator.
■ Freeze: Not suitable.
■ Microwave: Suitable.

1. Scrub mussels, remove beards.

3. Heat oil in pan, add shallots, cook, stirring, until shallots are soft; cool. Stir in rice, nuts, currants, herbs, rind, honey and half the butter; mix well.

Plate from Country Floors.

Cheese Crescent Pastries

80g butter, melted
1/3 cup (80ml) olive oil
1/4 cup (60ml) water
2 cups (300g) plain flour
1 egg, lightly beaten
FILLING
1 cup (200g) grated firm feta cheese
2 hard-boiled eggs, chopped
2 tablespoons finely chopped
    fresh parsley
40g packaged cream cheese

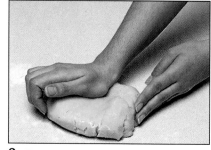

2. Turn dough onto lightly floured surface, knead gently until smooth. Cover, refrigerate 1 hour.

4. Drop slightly rounded teaspoons of filling into centre of each round. Fold over and pinch edges together decoratively to seal. Place pastries on greased oven trays, brush with egg. Bake in moderately hot oven about 15 minutes or until lightly browned.

1. Combine butter, oil and water in bowl. Add sifted flour, 1 tablespoon at a time, stirring to a smooth paste between additions. Continue adding flour until a soft dough is formed.

3. Divide pastry in half, roll each half between sheets of lightly floured baking paper until as thin as possible (pastry should be paper-thin and almost see-through). Cover, refrigerate 30 minutes. Cut 8cm rounds from pastry, re-roll pastry scraps. Refrigerate pastry between rolling if it becomes too soft to handle.

5. Filling: Combine all ingredients in bowl; mix well.
Makes about 45.

■ Recipe can be prepared
  a day ahead.
■ Storage: Covered, in refrigerator.
■ Freeze: Not suitable.
■ Microwave: Not suitable.

Baba Ghanoush

2 large (1kg) eggplants
1/4 cup (60ml) plain yogurt
2 tablespoons lemon juice
1 clove garlic, crushed
1/4 cup (60ml) tahini
2 teaspoons ground cumin
1/3 cup fresh coriander leaves

1. Pierce eggplants in several places with a skewer. Place whole eggplants on oven tray. Bake, uncovered, in hot oven about 1 hour or until soft; cool 15 minutes.

2. Peel eggplants, chop flesh roughly; discard skins.

3. Blend or process eggplant flesh with remaining ingredients until combined. Sprinkle with chopped parsley and serve with pita bread, if desired. Makes about 2 1/4 cups (560ml).

■ Recipe can be made 2 days ahead.
■ Storage: Covered, in refrigerator.
■ Freeze: Not suitable.
■ Microwave: Not suitable.

Plate and ceramic jar from The Bay Tree Kitchen Shop.

Lantern from Orson & Blake Collectables.

Spicy Lamb Pizzas

1 teaspoon dried yeast
1/2 teaspoon sugar
2/3 cup (160ml) warm water
1 1/2 cups (225g) plain flour
1/2 teaspoon salt
1/4 cup (60ml) olive oil
2 tablespoons pine nuts, toasted
1 tablespoon chopped fresh
    coriander leaves
LAMB TOPPING
2 teaspoons olive oil
250g minced lamb
1 small (80g) onion, finely chopped
1 clove garlic, crushed
1/2 teaspoon ground cinnamon
1 teaspoon ground cumin
1/2 teaspoon sambal oelek
1 small (90g) zucchini, grated
2 tablespoons tomato paste
1 large (250g) tomato,
    finely chopped

1. Combine yeast, sugar and 1/4 cup (60ml) of the water in small bowl, cover, stand in warm place about 20 minutes or until mixture is frothy.

2. Sift flour and salt into bowl. Stir in remaining water, yeast mixture and oil; mix to a soft dough. Knead dough on floured surface about 5 minutes or until smooth and elastic.

3. Place dough in oiled bowl, cover, stand in warm place about 1 hour or until dough is doubled in size. Turn dough onto lightly floured surface, knead until smooth. Divide dough into 18 pieces, roll each to a 10cm round.

4. Place rounds onto greased oven trays, top each with a tablespoon of lamb mixture, leaving a 1cm border. Sprinkle with nuts; brush edges with a little extra oil. Bake in moderately hot oven about 15 minutes or until cooked and browned. Sprinkle with coriander.

5. Lamb Topping: Heat oil in pan, add lamb, cook, stirring, until browned; remove from pan. Add onion, garlic, spices, sambal oelek and zucchini to same pan, cook, stirring, until onion is soft. Return lamb to pan, add paste and tomato, cook, stirring, about 5 minutes or until thickened slightly; cool.
Makes 18.

■ Topping can be made a day ahead.
■ Storage: Covered, in refrigerator.
■ Freeze: Uncooked pizzas suitable.
■ Microwave: Not suitable.

Mixed Vegetable Pickles

1 large (180g) carrot
4 (250g) gherkin cucumbers
250g cauliflower
1 medium (200g) red pepper
1 bunch (440g) baby turnips, trimmed
2 medium (260g) green tomatoes, quartered

PICKLING LIQUID
2½ cups (625ml) water
¼ cup (60g) rock salt
1 tablespoon sugar
2 bay leaves
2 small fresh red chillies
3 cups (750ml) white vinegar

1. Cut carrot and cucumbers into 2cm rounds. Cut cauliflower into small florets. Cut pepper into thin strips.

2. Layer vegetables and tomatoes in hot sterilised jar (3.5 litre/14 cup capacity). Pour in enough hot pickling liquid to cover vegetables; seal while hot.
Pickling Liquid: Combine water, salt, sugar, bay leaves and chillies in pan, stir over heat until boiling. Remove from heat, stir in vinegar.

■ Recipe best made 2 weeks ahead.
■ Storage: In refrigerator.
■ Freeze: Not suitable.
■ Microwave: Pickling liquid suitable.

Lamb and Eggplant Soup

2 small (460g) eggplants
40g ghee
6 (1.8kg) lamb shanks
1 medium (350g) leek, chopped
1½ cups (375ml) beef stock
2 litres (8 cups) water
1 cinnamon stick
1 large (500g) white sweet potato, chopped
1 teaspoon ground cumin
¼ cup chopped fresh parsley

2. Heat ghee in pan, add shanks in batches, cook until browned all over; drain on absorbent paper. Return shanks to pan with leek, stock and water, simmer, uncovered, 1 hour.

4. Add cinnamon, sweet potato and cumin to stock mixture in pan, simmer, covered, until sweet potato is soft. Discard cinnamon. Blend or process eggplant and sweet potato mixture in batches until smooth. Stir in meat and parsley. Return soup to pan, stir over heat until heated through.
Serves 6.

■ Recipe can be made a day ahead.
■ Storage: Covered, in refrigerator.
■ Freeze: Not suitable.
■ Microwave: Not suitable.

1. Pierce eggplants several times all over with skewer, place on oven tray. Bake in hot oven about 1 hour or until soft; cool. Peel eggplants, chop flesh roughly; discard skins.

3. Remove shanks from stock mixture; cool. Cut meat from bones; chop meat.

Blue plate and jug from Orson & Blake Collectables; bowl from The Bay Tree Kitchen Shop.

Hummus

2 teaspoons olive oil
1 medium (150g) onion, chopped
2 cloves garlic, crushed
1½ teaspoons ground cumin
2 x 425g cans chick peas, drained
½ cup (125ml) tahini
½ cup (125ml) lemon juice
1 tablespoon fresh coriander leaves
1 teaspoon ground hot paprika
¾ cup (180ml) buttermilk
SPICY LAVASH
480g packet lavash
2 tablespoons Cajun seasoning

1. Heat oil in pan, add onion and garlic, cook, stirring, until onion is soft. Add cumin, cook, stirring, until fragrant; cool 5 minutes.

2. Blend or process chick peas, tahini, juice, coriander, paprika, buttermilk and onion mixture until smooth. Spoon into serving bowl, drizzle with a little extra olive oil, if desired. Serve with spicy lavash.

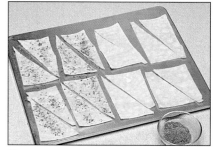

3. Spicy Lavash: Cut each lavash into 16 triangles, place in single layer on oven trays; sprinkle with seasoning. Toast in hot oven about 5 minutes or until crisp.
Makes about 1 litre (4 cups).

■ Hummus and spicy lavash can be made 3 days ahead.
■ Storage: Hummus, covered, in refrigerator. Spicy lavash, in airtight container.
■ Freeze: Not suitable.
■ Microwave: Onion mixture suitable.

Mushroom Spinach Cigars

2 tablespoons olive oil
2 small (200g) red Spanish onions,
    finely chopped
2 cloves garlic, crushed
1 teaspoon ground cinnamon
1/2 teaspoon ground allspice
1/2 teaspoon ground coriander
2 large (250g) flat mushrooms,
    finely chopped
1/2 bunch (250g) English spinach,
    finely shredded
2 teaspoons lemon juice
6 sheets fillo pastry
50g butter, melted

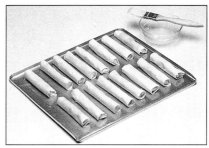

1. Heat oil in pan, add onions, garlic and spices, cook, stirring, until fragrant. Add mushrooms, cook, stirring, 5 minutes or until liquid has evaporated.

2. Stir in spinach and juice, cook, stirring, about 3 minutes or until spinach is wilted and any liquid has evaporated; cool to room temperature.

3. To prevent pastry from drying out, cover with a damp tea-towel. Layer 3 sheets of pastry together, brushing each with a little butter. Cut layered sheets into 8 squares. Place 1 tablespoon of mushroom mixture along 1 end of each square. Roll pastry over filling, fold in sides, roll up. Repeat with remaining pastry, more butter and remaining mushroom mixture.

4. Place cigars about 2cm apart on greased oven tray, brush with more butter. Bake in hot oven about 10 minutes or until browned.
Makes 16.

▪ Recipe best made just before serving. Mushroom mixture can be made a day ahead.
▪ Storage: Covered, in refrigerator.
▪ Freeze: Not suitable.
▪ Microwave: Not suitable.

Plate from Morris Home & Garden Wares; fabric from Joan Bowers Antiques.

Potato Cakes with Roasted Peppers

2 large (600g) old potatoes,
   peeled, grated
3 green shallots, finely chopped
1 egg yolk
¼ cup (30g) soya flour
1 teaspoon ground coriander
vegetable oil for shallow-frying
ROASTED PEPPERS
1 medium (200g) yellow pepper
1 medium (200g) red pepper
⅓ cup (55g) burghul
1½ cups finely chopped
   fresh parsley
⅓ cup (80ml) olive oil
¼ cup (60ml) lemon juice
DRESSING
1 cup (250ml) plain yogurt
2 teaspoons ground cumin
¾ teaspoon ground turmeric
1 teaspoon sugar

3. Roasted Peppers: Quarter peppers, remove seeds and membranes. Grill peppers, skin side up, until skin blisters and blackens; peel away skin, chop peppers finely.

4. Place burghul in small heatproof bowl, cover with boiling water, stand 20 minutes, drain. Place burghul between several sheets of absorbent paper, press paper to remove as much moisture as possible. Transfer burghul to bowl, add peppers and remaining ingredients; mix well.

1. Place potatoes between several sheets of absorbent paper, press paper to remove as much moisture as possible. Combine potatoes, shallots, egg yolk, flour and coriander in bowl; mix well.

5. Dressing: Combine all ingredients in bowl; mix well.
Serves 6.

2. Heat oil in pan, add ⅓ cup potato mixture in batches; flatten to 10cm rounds. Cook cakes slowly until browned underneath, turn, brown other side; drain on absorbent paper, keep warm. Serve topped with roasted peppers; drizzle with dressing.

- Potato cakes best made just before serving. Roasted peppers and dressing can be made a day ahead.
- Storage: Covered, separately, in refrigerator.
- Freeze: Not suitable.
- Microwave: Not suitable.

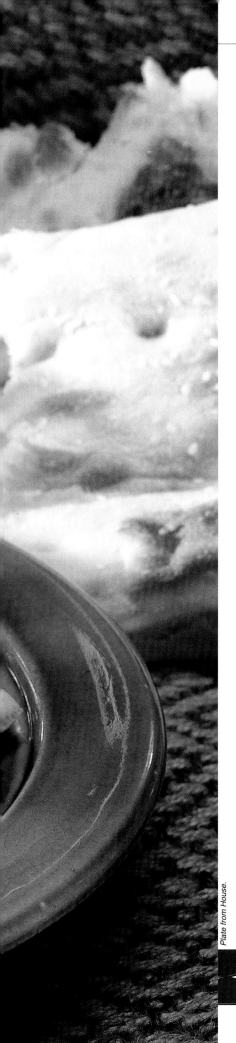

Plate from House.

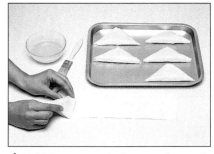

3. To prevent pastry from drying out, cover with damp tea-towel. Layer 2 sheets of pastry together, brushing each with butter. Cut layered sheets into 3 strips lengthways. Place a slightly rounded tablespoon of mixture at 1 end of each strip.

4. Fold 1 corner end of pastry diagonally across filling to other edge to form a triangle. Continue folding to end of strip, retaining triangular shape. Repeat with remaining pastry, more butter and remaining mixture. Place triangles on greased oven trays, brush with more butter. Bake in moderately hot oven about 8 minutes or until browned. Serve with tomato sauce.

Cloth from Joan Bowers Antiques.

Minted Beef and Pine Nut Pastries

2 teaspoons olive oil
1 small (80g) onion, chopped
2 cloves garlic, crushed
1 teaspoon ground cumin
1 teaspoon ground coriander
300g minced beef
2 tablespoons chopped fresh mint
2 tablespoons pine nuts
2 medium (400g) potatoes, chopped
1/2 cup (60g) grated tasty
     cheddar cheese
10 sheets fillo pastry
125g butter, melted
TOMATO SAUCE
2 teaspoons olive oil
1 small (80g) onion, chopped
2 cloves garlic, crushed
425g can tomatoes
1 tablespoon tomato paste
2 teaspoons brown sugar
2 tablespoons chopped fresh mint

1. Heat oil in pan, add onion, garlic and spices, cook, stirring, until onion is soft. Add beef, mint and nuts, cook, stirring, until beef is browned.

2. Boil, steam or microwave potatoes until soft. Mash potatoes until smooth, add cheese; mix well. Combine beef mixture and potatoes in bowl; mix well.

5. Tomato Sauce: Heat oil in pan, add onion and garlic, cook, stirring, until onion is soft. Add undrained crushed tomatoes, paste, sugar and mint, simmer, uncovered, about 5 minutes or until slightly thickened.
Makes 15.

■ Recipe best cooked just before serving. Filling and tomato sauce can be made a day ahead.
■ Storage: Covered, in refrigerator.
■ Freeze: Uncooked pastries suitable.
■ Microwave: Potatoes and tomato sauce suitable.

Preserved Lemons

You will need about 10 lemons and 7 limes for this recipe.

6 medium (850g) lemons
¼ cup (55g) coarse cooking salt
1 cup (250ml) lemon juice, approximately
1 cup (250ml) lime juice

1. Quarter lemons lengthways to within 5mm of the base.

2. Open out lemons, sprinkle cut surfaces with salt; reshape lemons.

3. Pack lemons very firmly into sterilised jar (1.5 litre/6 cup capacity), pour over enough combined juices to fill jar completely; seal jar.

To serve, remove and discard pulp from rind. Squeeze juice from rind, rinse rind well; slice thinly. Serve as part of a platter with olives, cubed feta cheese and sprinkled with olive oil. Rind can also be used in tagines, casseroles, with fish and in salads, etc.

■ Recipe best made 4 weeks ahead.
■ Storage: In a cool, dark place; turn jar every 2 days.
■ Freeze: Not suitable.

Yellow Split Pea Dip

1 cup (200g) yellow split peas
1 litre (4 cups) water
2 cloves garlic, bruised
1 medium (150g) onion, chopped
1 large (300g) potato, chopped
1/3 cup (80ml) olive oil
1/2 teaspoon ground cumin
1/2 teaspoon ground coriander

2. Boil, steam or microwave potato until tender, drain. Mash potato until smooth.

3. Blend or process pea mixture until smooth. Transfer to medium bowl, add potato, oil and spices; mix well. Drizzle with a little olive oil, serve warm or cold with Turkish bread, lemon wedges and olives, if desired.
Makes about 3½ cups (875ml).

■ Recipe can be made a day ahead.
■ Storage: Covered, in refrigerator.
■ Freeze: Not suitable.
■ Microwave: Potato suitable.

1. Rinse peas thoroughly under cold water; drain. Combine peas, water, garlic and onion in pan, simmer gently, uncovered, about 35 minutes or until peas are very soft.

Stuffed Vine Leaves

25 (120g) packaged vine leaves
   in brine
2 large (500g) tomatoes, sliced
1 cup (250ml) tomato puree
2 tablespoons olive oil
2 tablespoons lemon juice
1 cup (250ml) chicken stock
FILLING
1½ tablespoons olive oil
½ small (40g) onion, chopped
1 clove garlic, crushed
2 tablespoons white short-grain rice
1 tablespoon raisins, chopped
½ cup (125ml) water
1 teaspoon ground cinnamon
1 teaspoon ground coriander
2 tablespoons chopped fresh
   coriander leaves
1½ tablespoons flaked almonds,
   toasted, chopped
150g minced lamb

1. Place vine leaves in bowl, cover with cold water, stand 5 minutes; drain. Rinse leaves under cold water; drain well. Place leaves vein side up on board, place a rounded teaspoon of filling on each leaf, roll up firmly, folding in sides to enclose filling.

2. Cover base of 25cm heavy-based pan with tomato slices. Place rolls in single layer over tomatoes, pour over combined tomato puree, oil, juice and stock. Place a plate on top of rolls to keep rolls in position during cooking. Simmer, covered, over low heat about 1 hour or until cooked through.

3. Filling: Heat oil in pan, add onion and garlic, cook, stirring, until onion is soft. Add rice and raisins, mix well. Add water and spices, simmer, uncovered, about 5 minutes or until liquid is absorbed; cool. Stir in remaining ingredients.
Makes 25.

▓ Recipe can be made a day ahead.
▓ Storage: Covered, in refrigerator.
▓ Freeze: Not suitable.
▓ Microwave: Not suitable.

Plate from The Bay Tree Kitchen Shop.

Felafel

1 tablespoon olive oil
1 medium (150g) onion,
    roughly chopped
1 clove garlic, crushed
2 medium (400g) potatoes
1¼ cups (185g) frozen broad beans,
    thawed, peeled
½ teaspoon ground cinnamon
½ teaspoon ground cumin
¼ teaspoon chilli powder
⅓ cup fresh parsley leaves
plain flour
vegetable oil for deep-frying
YOGURT DIP
1 small (130g) green cucumber
¾ cup (180ml) plain yogurt
½ teaspoon ground cumin
2 teaspoons chopped fresh mint

1. Heat olive oil in pan, add onion and garlic, cook, stirring, until onion is soft. Boil, steam or microwave potatoes until soft, drain; mash until smooth.

2. Process onion mixture, potatoes, beans, spices and parsley until smooth.

3. Drop rounded teaspoons of mixture onto baking paper-covered trays, refrigerate 1 hour. Toss felafel in flour, roll into balls; flatten slightly. Deep-fry felafel in hot vegetable oil in batches until lightly browned; drain on absorbent paper. Serve with yogurt dip.

4. Yogurt Dip: Cut cucumber in half lengthways; remove seeds, finely chop cucumber. Combine cucumber with remaining ingredients in bowl; mix well. Makes about 30.

■ Felafel and yogurt dip can be made a day ahead.
■ Storage: Covered, separately, in refrigerator.
■ Freeze: Not suitable.
■ Microwave: Not suitable.

Main Courses

Here is a myriad of memorable meals. Lamb and chicken are favourites, especially when cooked in mouth-watering tagines, but subtly spiced vegetables and other meats also surprise and delight.

Chicken Tagine with Dates and Honey

9 (1kg) chicken thigh fillets
2 tablespoons olive oil
2 medium (300g) onions, finely sliced
4 cloves garlic, crushed
1 teaspoon cumin seeds
1 teaspoon ground coriander
1 teaspoon ground ginger
1 teaspoon ground turmeric
1 teaspoon ground cinnamon
1/2 teaspoon chilli powder
1/4 teaspoon ground nutmeg
1 1/2 cups (375ml) chicken stock
1 cup (250ml) water
1/2 cup (85g) seedless dates, halved
1/4 cup (60ml) honey
1/2 cup (80g) blanched almonds, toasted
1 tablespoon chopped fresh coriander leaves

2. Heat remaining oil in same pan, add onions, garlic and spices, cook, stirring, until onions are soft.

3. Return chicken to pan with stock and water, simmer, covered, 1 hour. Remove lid, simmer about 30 minutes or until mixture is thickened slightly and chicken is tender. Stir in dates, honey and nuts; sprinkle with fresh coriander. Serves 4 to 6.

- Chicken tagine can be made 3 hours ahead.
- Storage: Covered, in refrigerator.
- Freeze: Tagine suitable without nuts and coriander.
- Microwave: Not suitable.

1. Cut chicken into 3cm strips. Heat 1 tablespoon of the oil in pan, add chicken in batches, cook, stirring, until browned; drain on absorbent paper.

Plates and tagine from Francalia; small dish from Mr Brassman.

Plates from Francalia.

Beef with Olives and Coriander

1kg beef chuck steak
50g ghee
2 medium (300g) onions,
  finely chopped
2 teaspoons grated fresh ginger
1/2 teaspoon ground saffron
1 teaspoon ground cumin
1 teaspoon ground sweet paprika
1 tablespoon plain flour
1/4 cup (60ml) lemon juice
2 cups (500ml) beef stock
1 tablespoon chopped fresh
  coriander leaves
1 1/4 cups (200g) seedless
  black olives
3/4 cup (120g) seedless green olives

1. Cut beef into 3cm pieces. Heat ghee in pan, add beef in batches, cook, stirring, until browned all over; drain on absorbent paper.

2. Add onions and ginger to same pan, cook, stirring, until onions are soft.

3. Return beef to pan with saffron, cumin, paprika and flour, cook, stirring, until beef is well coated in spice mixture. Stir in juice and stock, simmer, covered, about 1 1/2 hours or until beef is tender. Just before serving, stir in coriander and olives.
Serves 6.

■ Recipe can be made a day ahead.
■ Storage: Covered, in refrigerator.
■ Freeze: Suitable.
■ Microwave: Not suitable.

Marinated Herbed Fish

2 cloves garlic, crushed
2 tablespoons olive oil
1½ tablespoons lemon juice
1 tablespoon chopped
  fresh rosemary
2 tablespoons chopped
  fresh parsley
¼ teaspoon dried crushed chillies
½ teaspoon sugar
1.5kg snapper
30g butter
1 medium (350g) leek, sliced
2 cloves garlic, crushed, extra
2 teaspoons chopped fresh thyme
2 teaspoons sugar, extra
6 medium (450g) egg tomatoes,
  quartered
400g can artichoke hearts in brine,
  drained, quartered

1. Combine garlic, oil, juice, herbies and sugar in small bowl; mix well.

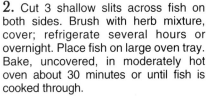

2. Cut 3 shallow slits across fish on both sides. Brush with herb mixture, cover; refrigerate several hours or overnight. Place fish on large oven tray. Bake, uncovered, in moderately hot oven about 30 minutes or until fish is cooked through.

3. Heat butter in pan, add leek, extra garlic and thyme, cook, stirring, until leek is soft. Add extra sugar, tomatoes and artichokes, cook, stirring, until heated through. Serve with fish.
Serves 4.

■ Recipe best cooked just
  before serving.
■ Freeze: Not suitable.
■ Microwave: Not suitable.

Serving fork and knife from Corso De' Fiori; tiles from Country Floors.

Chicken, Artichoke and Feta Pie

4 (680g) chicken breast fillets, halved
2 teaspoons ground cumin
1 teaspoon ground cinnamon
1 teaspoon ground turmeric
½ cup (125ml) chicken stock
2 tablespoons olive oil
2 medium (700g) leeks, sliced
2 x 280g jars artichoke hearts in oil, drained, chopped
½ teaspoon ground cinnamon, extra
200g feta cheese, crumbled
2 eggs, lightly beaten
¼ cup chopped fresh parsley
⅓ cup chopped fresh coriander leaves
12 sheets fillo pastry
80g butter, melted

3. To prevent pastry from drying out, cover with damp tea-towel until ready to use. Brush 1 sheet of pastry with some of the butter, place into greased 25cm round ovenproof dish (2.5 litre/10 cup capacity) with edges overhanging. Repeat with 5 more pastry sheets and more of the butter, overlapping pastry around dish.

1. Place chicken in shallow ovenproof dish (1.5 litre/6 cup capacity). Pour over combined spices and stock. Bake, covered, in moderate oven about 30 minutes or until tender. Remove chicken from dish, drain, finely chop; reserve ⅓ cup (80ml) juices in dish.

4. Spoon chicken mixture into dish, fold overhanging edges back onto filling; brush with more butter.

2. Heat oil in pan, add leeks, cook, stirring, about 10 minutes or until leeks are lightly browned and soft. Combine chicken, leeks, reserved juices, artichokes, extra cinnamon, cheese, eggs and herbs in large bowl; mix well.

5. Place 1 sheet of pastry over filling, brush with more butter. Repeat with remaining pastry sheets and butter, overlapping sheets around dish. Trim edges of pastry so they hang 2cm over edge of dish. Fold and tuck in overhanging pastry. Bake in moderately hot oven 20 minutes, reduce to moderate, bake about 20 minutes or until browned and heated through.
Serves 6.

■ Chicken mixture can be made a day ahead.
■ Storage: Covered, in refrigerator.
■ Freeze: Not suitable.
■ Microwave: Not suitable.

Copper tray from Mr Brassman.

Duck in Pomegranate Sauce

Because of their acidic nature, pomegranates should only be cooked in stainless steel or enamel pans to prevent discolouration.

2 x No.17 ducks
1 medium (320g) pomegranate
1 cup (250ml) water
1 tablespoon olive oil
1 medium (150g) onion, sliced
2 cloves garlic, crushed
1 teaspoon ground turmeric
1 teaspoon ground cinnamon
1 teaspoon ground cumin
1 teaspoon ground coriander
1 cup (250ml) chicken stock
1 tablespoon lemon juice
¼ cup (50g) brown sugar
2 tablespoons ground almonds

1. Place ducks on wire rack over large baking dish. Bake, uncovered, in moderately hot oven about 1 hour or until browned and just cooked. Remove from oven, cover; stand 30 minutes.

2. Cut pomegranate in half; scoop out seeds, reserve ¼ cup (60ml) seeds. Combine remaining seeds and water in stainless steel or enamel pan, bring to boil; strain.

3. Heat oil in stainless steel or enamel pan, add onion, garlic and spices, cook, stirring, until onion is soft. Add pomegranate liquid, stock, juice, sugar and almonds, cook, stirring, over heat until mixture boils and thickens slightly.

4. Place a duck on board, cut through breastbone, using poultry shears. Cut on either side of backbone; remove backbone.

5. Remove breastbone and ribcage from each half of duck. Cut each half into 2 pieces. Repeat with remaining duck. Grill duck, skin side up, until skin is crisp. Place duck pieces on serving plate, pour over sauce, top with reserved pomegranate seeds then chopped pistachios and coriander leaves, if desired.
Serves 4 to 6.

■ Recipe can be made 3 hours ahead.
■ Storage: Covered, in refrigerator.
■ Freeze: Not suitable.
■ Microwave: Not suitable.

Plate and vase from The Bay Tree Kitchen Shop.

Roast Lamb with Spiced Yogurt Crust

2kg leg of lamb
4 cloves garlic, quartered
2 teaspoons ground sweet paprika
2 teaspoons ground cumin
1 teaspoon ground turmeric
1 teaspoon ground coriander
1 teaspoon ground black pepper
1/2 teaspoon ground cardamom
1/2 teaspoon saffron threads
2 teaspoons grated lemon rind
2 cups (500ml) plain yogurt

1. Make 16 x 4cm deep cuts into lamb, press garlic into cuts.

2. Combine ground spices, saffron, rind and yogurt in bowl; mix well. Spread spiced yogurt over lamb, cover; refrigerate overnight.

3. Place lamb on wire rack in baking dish, add enough water to cover base of baking dish. Bake, uncovered, in moderate oven about 1½ hours or until crust is browned and lamb tender. Remove from oven, cover loosely with foil; stand 30 minutes before carving. Serve with char-grilled tomatoes and vegetables, if desired.
Serves 6 to 8.

■ Recipe must be prepared
  a day ahead.
■ Storage: Covered, in refrigerator.
■ Freeze: Not suitable.
■ Microwave: Not suitable.

Marinated Tuna Kebabs

Soak bamboo skewers in water for several hours or overnight to prevent them from burning.

1kg piece of fresh tuna
MARINADE
½ cup fresh parsley sprigs
½ cup fresh coriander leaves
3 cloves garlic, bruised
1 teaspoon ground cinnamon
1 teaspoon ground cumin
1 teaspoon ground sweet paprika
1 teaspoon ground coriander
½ cup (125ml) lemon juice
¼ cup (60ml) olive oil
1 teaspoon grated lemon rind

1. Cut tuna into 3cm cubes. Combine tuna and marinade in large bowl, mix well; cover, refrigerate overnight.

2. Thread tuna onto 8 skewers, grill or barbecue until cooked as desired, turning once during cooking. Serve with lemon wedges, if desired.
Marinade: Blend or process all ingredients until smooth.
Makes 8.

■ Recipe best prepared a day ahead.
■ Storage: Covered, in refrigerator.
■ Freeze: Uncooked marinated tuna suitable.
■ Microwave: Not suitable.

Plate and spice pot from Francalia; copper tray from Mr Brassman.

Veal Shanks with Caramelised Apples

We found best results were obtained by cooking this recipe on top of the stove.

2 tablespoons olive oil
6 (4kg) veal shanks
2 small (160g) onions, halved
3 cloves garlic, bruised
2 cinnamon sticks
2cm piece peeled fresh ginger
2 fresh coriander roots
3 cups (750ml) beef stock
1 cup (250ml) orange juice
2 teaspoons cornflour
1 tablespoon water

CARAMELISED APPLES
60g butter
6 medium (900g) apples, peeled, cored, sliced
1/4 cup (50g) brown sugar
1/4 cup (20g) flaked almonds

1. Heat oil in large heavy-based baking dish, add veal in batches, cook until well browned all over.

2. Return veal to dish with onions, garlic, cinnamon, ginger, coriander, stock and juice, simmer, covered tightly, about 1½ hours or until veal is tender and starting to fall off bones. Remove veal from dish, cool 10 minutes. Cut meat from bones; keep meat warm.

3. Strain juices from dish into clean pan, simmer, uncovered, about 20 minutes or until reduced to 1½ cups (375ml). Add blended cornflour and water, stir over heat until sauce boils and thickens slightly. Serve sauce over veal with caramelised apples. Top with shredded orange rind and parsley, if desired.

4. Caramelised Apples: Melt butter in pan, add apples, cook, stirring, until apples are browned. Add sugar, cook, stirring gently, about 5 minutes or until apple mixture starts to caramelise. Stir in almonds.
Serves 6 to 8.

▪ Veal can be cooked a day ahead. Caramelised apples best made just before serving.
▪ Storage: Covered, in refrigerator.
▪ Freeze: Veal suitable.
▪ Microwave: Not suitable.

Plate from Country Floors.

Plate from Country Floors.

1. Combine chicken, shallots, nuts, fruit and spices in bowl; mix well. Loosen skin of duck by sliding fingers between skin and meat, ensuring skin remains attached along edge. Push quarter of the chicken mixture under skin of each breast.

2. Place duck skin side down in heated pan, cook about 3 minutes or until skin is browned.

3. Transfer duck, skin side up, to wire rack in baking dish. Bake, uncovered, in moderate oven about 25 minutes or until duck is tender. Serve duck sliced with orange sauce.
Orange Sauce: Combine juice, stock, cumin and blended cornflour and water in pan, stir over heat until mixture boils and thickens; stir in coriander.
Serves 4.

■ Recipe can be prepared
   a day ahead.
■ Storage: Covered, in refrigerator.
■ Freeze: Seasoned duck suitable.
■ Microwave: Not suitable.

Duck Breast with Pistachio Seasoning

150g chicken mince
2 green shallots, finely chopped
¼ cup (35g) pistachios,
   toasted, chopped
2 tablespoons chopped
   dried apricots
2 tablespoons chopped glace figs
2 teaspoons ground cumin
1 teaspoon caraway seeds
4 (600g) duck breast fillets

ORANGE SAUCE
½ cup (125ml) orange juice
½ cup (125ml) chicken stock
½ teaspoon ground cumin
1 tablespoon cornflour
1 tablespoon water
1 tablespoon chopped fresh
   coriander leaves

Minted Veal with Baby Squash

2 tablespoons olive oil
12 (2kg) veal loin chops
2 medium (300g) onions, sliced
3 cloves garlic, crushed
2 teaspoons ground turmeric
4 cardamom pods, bruised
1 teaspoon ground nutmeg
1 teaspoon grated lemon rind
1 tablespoon tomato paste
2 tablespoons chopped fresh mint
2 cups (500ml) beef stock
200g baby yellow squash, halved
1 tablespoon cornflour
2 tablespoons water

1. Heat oil in pan, add veal in batches, cook until browned all over; remove.

2. Add onions, garlic and spices to same pan, cook, stirring, until onion is soft. Add rind, paste, mint, stock and veal, simmer, covered, about 30 minutes or until veal is tender.

3. Add squash, simmer, uncovered, about 10 minutes or until squash are tender. Add blended cornflour and water, stir over heat until mixture boils and thickens.
Serves 6 to 8.

China from Joan Bowers Antiques.

▨ Recipe can be made a day ahead.
▨ Storage: Covered, in refrigerator.
▨ Freeze: Suitable.
▨ Microwave: Not suitable.

Spicy Roasted Spatchcocks

4 x No. 5 spatchcocks
2 teaspoons ground sweet paprika
2 cloves garlic, crushed
1 teaspoon cumin seeds
2 teaspoons yellow mustard seeds
1 tablespoon chopped fresh
    coriander leaves
2 green shallots, chopped
1/3 cup (80ml) mango chutney
2 tablespoons olive oil
VINAIGRETTE
2 tablespoons olive oil
1 tablespoon lemon juice
1/2 teaspoon chopped fresh
    rosemary
1/4 teaspoon sugar

4. Combine spatchcocks in bowl with paprika, garlic, seeds, coriander, shallots, chutney and oil; mix well. Cover, refrigerate overnight.

1. Using poultry shears, cut along both sides of spatchcock backbones; remove and discard backbones.

5. Place spatchcocks on wire rack over baking dish. Bake, uncovered, in hot oven about 30 minutes or until spatchcocks are tender, brushing with remaining marinade several times during cooking. Serve spatchcocks on watercress sprigs, if desired. Drizzle with vinaigrette.

2. Place spatchcocks, skin side down, on board. Scrape meat away from rib cage; remove rib cage. Cut through thigh and wing joints without cutting skin.

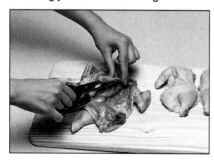

3. Scrape meat from breastbones; remove breastbones; Cut spatchcocks in half.

6. **Vinaigrette:** Combine all ingredients in jar; shake well.
Serves 4.

■ Recipe can be prepared
   a day ahead.
■ Storage: Covered, in refrigerator.
■ Freeze: Uncooked marinated
   spatchcocks suitable.
■ Microwave: Not suitable.

Plate and bowl from Accoutrement; basket from Orson & Blake Collectables.

2. Thread lamb onto skewers. Heat oil in pan, add kebabs in batches, cook until browned all over and cooked through. Serve with tomato sauce.

3. **Marinade:** Process all ingredients until well combined.

4. **Tomato Sauce:** Combine undrained crushed tomatoes with remaining ingredients in small pan, simmer, uncovered, about 5 minutes or until slightly thickened.
Serves 4.

- Recipe can be prepared a day ahead.
- Storage: Covered, in refrigerator.
- Freeze: Not suitable.
- Microwave: Not suitable.

Plate from Morris Home & Garden Wares.

Marinated Lemony Lamb Kebabs

1kg boneless lamb
1 tablespoon olive oil

MARINADE
2 large (400g) onions, chopped
2 cloves garlic, crushed
½ cup (125ml) olive oil
¼ cup (60ml) lemon juice
1 teaspoon ground cumin
½ teaspoon ground ginger
1 teaspoon ground coriander

TOMATO SAUCE
425g can tomatoes
1 small fresh red chilli,
    finely chopped
½ teaspoon ground cumin
¼ teaspoon ground cinnamon

1. Cut lamb into 3cm cubes. Combine lamb and marinade in bowl, cover; refrigerate several hours or overnight.

Lamb and Chick Pea Casserole

1kg diced lamb
1 teaspoon ground sweet paprika
1 teaspoon ground cumin
50g ghee
2 large (400g) onions, sliced
½ teaspoon ground turmeric
2 x 425g cans tomatoes
2 teaspoons sugar
300g can chick peas, drained
2 teaspoons chopped fresh thyme
1 tablespoon chopped fresh parsley

1. Combine lamb, paprika and cumin in bowl, mix well, cover; refrigerate several hours or overnight.

2. Heat ghee in pan, add lamb mixture and onions, cook, stirring, until onions are soft; stir in turmeric.

3. Add undrained crushed tomatoes and sugar, simmer, covered, about 40 minutes or until lamb is just tender. Add chick peas and herbs, simmer, uncovered, about 10 minutes or until lamb is tender and sauce thickened slightly. Serves 4 to 6.

Plates from Francalia.

■ Recipe can be made a day ahead.
■ Storage: Covered, in refrigerator.
■ Freeze: Suitable.
■ Microwave: Not suitable.

Veal and Ricotta Calsones

3 eggs
1¾ cups (260g) plain flour
2 tablespoons olive oil
flaked kefalograviera cheese

FILLING
1 tablespoon olive oil
1 small (80g) onion, chopped
1 clove garlic, crushed
½ teaspoon garam masala
1 teaspoon ground cumin
100g minced veal
2 tablespoons chopped
    fresh parsley
½ cup (100g) ricotta cheese
1 tablespoon pistachios, toasted,
    finely chopped

TOMATO SAUCE
1 tablespoon olive oil
1 medium (150g) onion, chopped
1 clove garlic, crushed
½ teaspoon ground cumin
8 medium (1kg) tomatoes, peeled,
    seeded, chopped
½ cup (125ml) tomato paste
1 cup (250ml) chicken stock
1 cinnamon stick
1 teaspoon sugar

1. Process eggs, flour and oil until mixture forms a ball.

2. Knead dough on lightly floured surface until smooth. Divide dough into 4 pieces, roll each piece through pasta machine set on thickest setting. Fold dough in half, roll through machine; repeat rolling several times, dusting dough with extra flour when necessary.

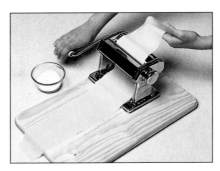

3. Roll dough through machine, adjusting setting so dough becomes thinner with each roll, dust with extra flour, when necessary. Roll to second thinnest setting (1mm thick), making sure dough is at least 12cm wide.

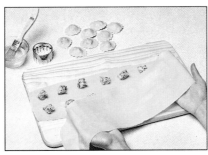

4. Place teaspoons of filling 4cm apart over 1 sheet of pasta. Lightly brush another sheet of pasta with water, place over filling; press firmly between filling. Cut out calsones, using 5.5cm round fluted cutter. Repeat with remaining pasta sheets and filling.

5. Add calsones in batches to large pan of boiling water, boil, uncovered, about 5 minutes or until calsones are just tender; drain. Serve with tomato sauce, topped with cheese.

6. Filling: Heat oil in pan, add onion, garlic and spices, cook, stirring, until onion is soft. Add veal, cook, stirring, until veal is browned. Remove from heat, stir in parsley, cheese and nuts.

7. Tomato Sauce: Heat oil in pan, add onion, garlic and cumin, cook, stirring, until onion is soft. Stir in tomatoes, paste, stock, cinnamon and sugar, simmer, covered, about 15 minutes or until sauce thickens. Discard cinnamon.
Serves 4.

- Filling and sauce can be prepared a day ahead.
- Storage: Covered, separately, in refrigerator.
- Freeze: Uncooked calsones suitable.
- Microwave: Tomato sauce suitable.

Eggplants with Pumpkin and Feta

You will need to cook 1/3 cup (65g) rice for this recipe.

4 medium (1.2kg) eggplants, halved
coarse cooking salt
1/4 cup (60ml) olive oil
200g piece pumpkin, finely chopped
1 small (80g) onion, finely chopped
2 cloves garlic, crushed
1 teaspoon ground cumin
2 tablespoons brown sugar
1 cup cooked long-grain rice
2 tablespoons chopped fresh
** coriander leaves**
1/3 cup (50g) hazelnuts,
** toasted, chopped**
100g feta cheese, crumbled

1. Sprinkle cut surface of eggplants with salt, place on wire rack over dish, stand 30 minutes. Rinse eggplants, pat dry with absorbent paper. Brush cut surface of eggplants with half the oil, place on wire rack over baking dish. Bake, uncovered, in moderate oven about 40 minutes or until eggplants are tender; cool 10 minutes.

2. Scoop flesh from eggplants, leaving 5mm shells. Chop eggplant flesh.

3. Heat remaining oil in pan, add pumpkin, onion, garlic and cumin, cook, stirring, until pumpkin is just tender. Stir in eggplant flesh, sugar, rice, coriander and nuts.

4. Divide pumpkin mixture between eggplant shells, place on oven tray; top with cheese. Bake, uncovered, in moderate oven about 30 minutes or until cheese is lightly browned.
Serves 4.

■ Recipe can be prepared
   a day ahead.
■ Storage: Covered, in refrigerator.
■ Freeze: Not suitable.
■ Microwave: Suitable.

Lamb, Eggplant and Prune Tagine

2 medium (600g) eggplants
coarse cooking salt
1/4 cup (60ml) olive oil
1kg diced lamb
1/2 teaspoon ground cinnamon
2 teaspoons ground cumin
1/2 teaspoon ground ginger
1 teaspoon ground turmeric
2 cloves garlic, crushed
1 large (200g) onion, finely chopped
2 3/4 cups (680ml) water
2 strips lemon rind
1 cinnamon stick
3/4 cup (125g) seedless prunes,
   halved
1/2 cup (80g) blanched almonds,
   toasted
1 tablespoon honey
2 tablespoons chopped fresh
   coriander leaves
2 teaspoons sesame seeds, toasted

1. Cut eggplants into 1cm slices, place in colander, sprinkle with salt; stand 30 minutes. Rinse slices under cold water, drain, cut into quarters.

2. Heat oil in pan, add lamb and ground spices, cook, stirring, until lamb is browned all over; remove from pan. Add garlic and onion to pan, cook, stirring, until onion is soft. Stir in water, rind and cinnamon stick. Return lamb to pan, simmer, covered, about 1 hour or until lamb is just tender.

Tagine from The Bay Tree Kitchen Shop.

3. Stir in prunes, nuts, honey, coriander and eggplants, simmer, covered, about 30 minutes or until eggplants are tender. Discard cinnamon stick and rind. Serve tagine sprinkled with seeds. Serves 6.

- Recipe can be made a day ahead.
- Storage: Covered, in refrigerator.
- Freeze: Suitable.
- Microwave: Not suitable.

Lamb with Olive Couscous Seasoning

Ask your butcher to bone the leg of lamb for you.

1.5kg boned leg of lamb
1 tablespoon olive oil
1/3 cup (80ml) orange juice
1/2 teaspoon ground cinnamon
1/4 cup (60ml) honey
2 cloves garlic, crushed
1 1/2 tablespoons cornflour
2 cups (500ml) beef stock
OLIVE COUSCOUS SEASONING
1/2 cup (100g) couscous
1/2 cup (125ml) boiling water
20g butter
1 small (80g) onion, chopped
1 teaspoon ground cumin
2 tablespoons flaked almonds, toasted
1 small (130g) apple, peeled, cored, chopped
1 tablespoon brown sugar
1/4 cup (40g) chopped seedless black olives

3. Combine juice, cinnamon, honey and garlic in small bowl; brush a little juice mixture over lamb. Return lamb to moderate oven for about 30 minutes or until tender; brush with remaining juice mixture several times during cooking. Remove lamb from dish; stand 10 minutes before carving.

4. Blend cornflour with a little of the stock in small bowl, stir into juices in baking dish with remaining stock. Stir over heat until mixture boils and thickens, simmer, uncovered, 5 minutes; strain. Serve sauce with lamb.

1. Place lamb on board, pound with meat mallet until lamb is an even thickness. Place olive couscous seasoning in centre of lamb; roll up from short side to enclose seasoning.

2. Secure lamb with skewers, tie with string at 2cm intervals. Place lamb on wire rack in baking dish, brush with oil. Bake, uncovered, in moderate oven 2 hours.

5. **Olive Couscous Seasoning:** Combine couscous and water in heatproof bowl, stand 5 minutes or until all the liquid has been absorbed. Heat butter in pan, add onion, cook, stirring, until onion is soft. Add cumin, nuts, apple, sugar and olives, cook, stirring, few minutes or until apple is softened slightly. Stir in couscous; cool.
Serves 6.

■ Recipe can be prepared a day ahead.
■ Storage: Covered, in refrigerator.
■ Freeze: Not suitable.
■ Microwave: Not suitable.

Embroidered cloth from Anokhi.

2. Heat oil in pan, add leek, garlic and spices, cook, stirring, until leek is soft and liquid evaporated. Transfer mixture to large bowl, add spinach, herbs, nuts, cheese and eggs; mix well.

3. To prevent pastry from drying out, cover with a damp tea-towel until you are ready to use it. Layer 2 sheets of pastry together, brushing each with a little of the butter. Cut layered sheets in half lengthways. Place 1/3 cup spinach mixture at 1 end of each strip.

4. Fold 1 corner end of pastry diagonally across filling to other edge to form a triangle. Continue folding to end of strip, retaining triangular shape. Brush triangle with a little more butter. Repeat with remaining pastry, filling and butter. Place triangles on greased oven trays. Bake in moderately hot oven about 15 minutes or until browned.
Makes 12.

■ Filling can be made a day ahead.
■ Storage: Covered, in refrigerator.
■ Freeze: Uncooked triangles suitable.
■ Microwave: Spinach suitable.

Spinach, Leek and Cheese Pastries

2 bunches (1kg) English spinach, chopped
2 tablespoons water
2 tablespoons olive oil
1 large (500g) leek, chopped
4 cloves garlic, crushed
1/2 teaspoon ground cumin
1/2 teaspoon ground cinnamon
1/4 cup chopped fresh dill
1/2 cup chopped fresh parsley
1/2 cup (80g) pine nuts, toasted
500g feta cheese, crumbled
2 eggs, lightly beaten
12 sheets fillo pastry
100g butter, melted

1. Combine spinach and water in large pan, simmer, covered, few minutes or until spinach is wilted, drain; squeeze out excess liquid.

Wooden box from Morris Home & Garden Wares.

Kibbi

1 cup (160g) burghul
600g minced lamb
1 medium (150g) onion, grated
1 teaspoon ground allspice
1 teaspoon ground oregano
1 tablespoon olive oil
1 tablespoon water
vegetable oil for shallow-frying
FILLING
2 teaspoons olive oil
1 small (80g) onion, finely chopped
1 tablespoon pine nuts
1 tablespoon slivered almonds
100g minced lamb
½ teaspoon ground allspice
½ teaspoon ground oregano
1 tablespoon chopped fresh mint

1. Place burghul in bowl, cover with cold water, stand 15 minutes. Drain burghul, rinse under cold water, drain; squeeze to remove excess moisture.

2. Combine burghul with lamb, onion, allspice, oregano, olive oil and water in bowl; mix well.

3. Shape ¼ cups of lamb mixture into balls, using damp hands. Hollow out centres of meatballs, using your thumb. Place rounded teaspoons of filling into hollowed centres of meatballs. Shape meatballs into ovals, using damp hands.

4. Shallow-fry kibbi in hot oil in batches until browned all over and cooked through; drain on absorbent paper.

5. Filling: Heat oil in pan, add onion, cook, stirring, until onion is soft. Add nuts, cook, stirring, until lightly browned. Add lamb, allspice and oregano, cook, stirring, until lamb is browned. Stir in mint.
Makes about 16.

■ Recipe can be prepared
　a day ahead.
■ Storage: Covered, in refrigerator.
■ Freeze: Cooked kibbi suitable.
■ Microwave: Not suitable.

Spicy Lamb Racks with Quince

6 medium (2kg) quinces
2 tablespoons olive oil
60g butter
1 clove garlic, crushed
1 teaspoon ground cumin
1 teaspoon coriander seeds, crushed
2/3 cup (160ml) dry white wine
1/4 cup (50g) brown sugar
SPICY LAMB RACKS
2 tablespoons olive oil
1 tablespoon honey
2 teaspoons ground cumin
1½ teaspoons ground coriander
1 teaspoon ground turmeric
½ teaspoon ground allspice
¼ teaspoon cayenne pepper
6 racks (1kg) lamb (3 cutlets in each)

1. Peel quinces, cut each quince into 8 pieces; remove cores.

2. Heat oil, butter, garlic and spices in large baking dish, cook, stirring, until fragrant. Add quinces, cook, stirring, about 5 minutes or until lightly browned. Stir in wine and sugar. Bake, uncovered, in moderate oven about 45 minutes or until quinces are pale pink and lightly browned, stirring occasionally.

3. Place spicy lamb racks on top of quinces in baking dish. Bake, uncovered, in moderate oven about 15 minutes or until lamb is tender.

4. Spicy Lamb Racks: Combine 1 tablespoon of the oil with honey and spices in bowl; mix well. Brush lamb with spice mixture, cover; refrigerate several hours or overnight.

5. Heat remaining oil in pan, add lamb in batches, cook until browned all over. Serves 6.

▓ Lamb can be prepared a day ahead.
▓ Storage: Covered, in refrigerator.
▓ Freeze: Not suitable.
▓ Microwave: Not suitable.

Setting from Home & Garden on the Mall.

Braised Beef with Kidney Beans

1kg beef chuck steak
2 tablespoons olive oil
2 medium (300g) onions,
finely chopped
2 cloves garlic, finely sliced
2 teaspoons ground oregano
1 teaspoon ground turmeric
2 teaspoons ground cumin
425g can tomatoes
2 cups (500ml) beef stock
1/4 cup (60ml) tomato paste
2 bay leaves
1 cinnamon stick
6 baby (240g) new potatoes, halved
2 small (400g) leeks, thinly sliced
290g can red kidney beans,
rinsed, drained
2 tablespoons chopped fresh
coriander leaves
2 tablespoons chopped fresh dill

1. Cut beef into 4cm pieces. Heat oil in pan, add beef in batches, cook, stirring, until browned. Transfer beef to oven-proof dish (2.5 litre/10 cup capacity).

2. Add onions to same pan, cook, stirring, until soft. Add garlic and ground spices, cook, stirring, until fragrant. Stir in undrained crushed tomatoes, stock and paste; bring to boil.

3. Pour tomato mixture over beef in dish, add bay leaves and cinnamon stick. Bake, covered, in moderately hot oven 1 hour.

4. Remove lid, bake in moderately hot oven 30 minutes. Stir in potatoes and leeks. Bake, uncovered, in moderately hot oven about 20 minutes or until beef and potatoes are tender. Discard cinnamon and bay leaves. Stir in beans and herbs.
Serves 6.

■ Recipe can be made a day ahead.
■ Storage: Covered, in refrigerator.
■ Freeze: Suitable.
■ Microwave: Not suitable.

Setting from The Pacific East India Co.

2. Add nuts and parsley, mix well; cover, refrigerate 30 minutes.

3. Roll tablespoons of mixture into ovals. Thread 3 ovals onto each skewer.

4. Cook kofta in greased heated griddle pan (or grill or barbecue) in batches until browned and cooked through. Makes about 14.

- Recipe can be prepared a day ahead.
- Storage: Covered, in refrigerator.
- Freeze: Not suitable.
- Microwave: Not suitable.

Plates from The Bay Tree Kitchen Shop.

Lamb Kofta

Soak bamboo skewers in water several hours or overnight to prevent them from burning.

750g minced lamb
1 large (200g) onion, finely chopped
2 cloves garlic, crushed
1/4 teaspoon ground cloves
1/4 teaspoon ground nutmeg
1/4 teaspoon ground hot paprika
1/2 teaspoon ground cumin
1/2 teaspoon ground coriander
1 teaspoon finely grated lemon rind
1/4 cup (40g) pine nuts, finely chopped
1/2 cup finely chopped fresh parsley

1. Combine lamb, onion, garlic, spices and rind in bowl; mix well.

Wooden tray from from Corso De´ Fiori; wooden bowl from Orson & Blake Collectables.

Spicy Tomato Coriander Prawns

1kg uncooked medium prawns
2 teaspoons ground hot paprika
1 teaspoon coriander seeds,
   crushed
1 teaspoon ground turmeric
1 teaspoon ground cumin
1 teaspoon cracked black pepper
1/4 teaspoon ground cloves
1/4 teaspoon ground cardamom
1/4 cup (60ml) water
1 tablespoon light olive oil
2 medium (300g) onions, sliced
2 large (500g) tomatoes, chopped
2 tablespoons finely shredded fresh
   coriander leaves

1. Shell and devein prawns, leaving tails intact. Combine spices and water in small bowl; mix well.

2. Heat oil in pan, add onions, cook, stirring, 2 minutes. Add spice mixture, cook, stirring, until fragrant.

3. Add prawns and tomatoes, cook, stirring, until prawns are just tender. Remove from heat; stir in fresh coriander. Serves 4 to 6.

▓ Recipe best made close to serving.
▓ Freeze: Not suitable.
▓ Microwave: Suitable.

Salads & Vegetables

Vegetables feature prominently in most meals, in every country, throughout the Middle East. A huge variety of vegetables is used, eaten raw or cooked, stuffed or pickled. Make the most of a plentiful harvest and taste the delicious difference.

Spicy Potato and Coriander Salad

1kg baby new potatoes, halved
1½ tablespoons olive oil
1 medium (170g) red Spanish onion, chopped
3 cloves garlic, crushed
3 teaspoons ground cumin
1½ teaspoons ground coriander
1 teaspoon ground sweet paprika
½ teaspoon ground turmeric
¼ teaspoon ground cinnamon
½ cup chopped fresh coriander leaves
DRESSING
⅓ cup (80ml) lemon juice
¼ cup (60ml) olive oil
½ teaspoon sambal oelek
1 teaspoon sugar
¼ teaspoon cracked black pepper

2. Heat oil in pan, add onion, garlic and ground spices, cook, stirring, until onion is soft. Add potatoes and coriander, cook, stirring, about 5 minutes or until potatoes are well coated and heated through. Combine potato mixture and dressing in bowl; mix well.

1. Add potatoes to pan of boiling water, simmer, uncovered, until tender; drain.

3. Dressing: Combine all ingredients in jar; shake well.
Serves 4 to 6.

■ Recipe can be prepared a day ahead.
■ Storage: Covered, in refrigerator.
■ Freeze: Not suitable.
■ Microwave: Potatoes suitable.

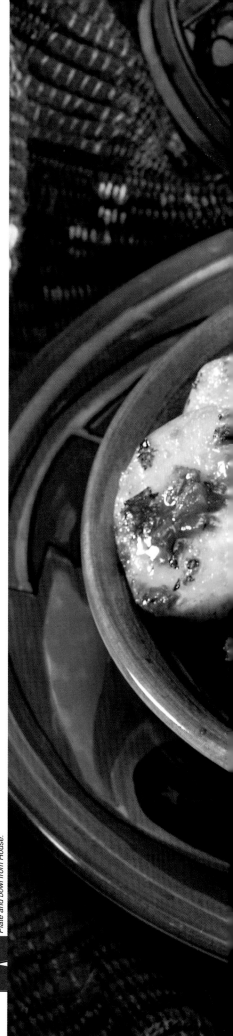

Plate and bowl from House.

2. Heat half the oil in pan, add onions, cook, stirring occasionally, about 15 minutes or until onions are browned; remove from pan.

3. Heat remaining oil in same pan, add okra, garlic and spices, cook, stirring, about 5 minutes or until okra is fragrant and lightly browned.

4. Return onions to pan with undrained crushed tomatoes and stock, simmer, uncovered, about 40 minutes, stirring occasionally, or until okra is very soft and tomato mixture is thickened. Serves 4 to 6.

■ Recipe best made close to serving.
■ Freeze: Not suitable.
■ Microwave: Not suitable.

Okra with Baby Onions and Tomato
700g okra
¼ cup (60ml) olive oil
12 (300g) baby onions, halved
2 cloves garlic, crushed
2 teaspoons ground cumin
1 teaspoon ground cinnamon
½ teaspoon ground allspice
425g can tomatoes
2 cups (500ml) chicken stock

1. Trim stems from okra, taking care not to puncture pods.

Plate from Country Floors.

Fattoush

2 large pita pocket breads
2 tablespoons olive oil
1 clove garlic, crushed
2 small (260g) green cucumbers, thinly sliced
4 medium (300g) egg tomatoes, quartered
1 medium (200g) red pepper, chopped
6 green shallots, chopped
2 tablespoons chopped fresh parsley
1 tablespoon chopped fresh mint
DRESSING
1/3 cup (80ml) lemon juice
1/4 cup (60ml) light olive oil
1 clove garlic, crushed
1 teaspoon ground sweet paprika
1/4 teaspoon ground cumin
1/4 teaspoon freshly ground black pepper

1. Brush each side of bread with combined oil and garlic, place bread on oven trays. Toast in moderately hot oven about 15 minutes or until crisp, cool. Break bread into pieces.

2. Combine cucumbers, tomatoes, pepper, shallots and herbs in bowl. Just before serving, add bread; drizzle fattoush with dressing.
Dressing: Combine all ingredients in jar; shake well.
Serves 4.

■ Bread and dressing can be prepared a day ahead.
■ Storage: Bread, in airtight container. Dressing, covered, in refrigerator.
■ Freeze: Not suitable.
■ Microwave: Not suitable.

Tabbouleh

²/₃ cup (110g) burghul
6 cups firmly packed flat-leaf
    parsley, coarsely chopped
½ cup coarsely chopped fresh mint
5 large (1.25kg) tomatoes, chopped
2 medium (300g) onions, chopped
2 green shallots, finely chopped
¾ cup (180ml) olive oil
¾ cup (180ml) fresh lemon juice

1. Cover burghul with cold water, stand 15 minutes. Drain, press as much water as possible from burghul. Place burghul in large bowl.

2. Add remaining ingredients to bowl, mix gently until combined.
Serves 6 to 8.

▪ Recipe best made on day of serving.
▪ Freeze: Not suitable.

Orange, Date and Almond Salad

4 large (1.2kg) oranges
1/3 cup (50g) dried apricots, halved
2 tablespoons blanched almonds, toasted
2 tablespoons chopped fresh mint
SYRUP MIXTURE
1 cup (250ml) water
2 star anise
1 cinnamon stick
6 cloves
2 tablespoons honey
1/2 cup (95g) sliced dried figs
1/2 cup (85g) seedless dates, halved

1. Peel oranges thickly, remove any white pith, cut between membranes into segments. Combine orange segments, apricots, almonds and mint in bowl, add syrup mixture; mix well.

2. **Syrup Mixture:** Combine water, star anise, cinnamon, cloves and honey in small pan, simmer, uncovered, about 10 minutes or until thickened and slightly syrupy. Add figs and dates; cool. Discard star anise, cinnamon and cloves.
Serves 4.

■ Recipe can be made a day ahead.
■ Storage: Covered, in refrigerator.
■ Freeze: Not suitable.
■ Microwave: Not suitable.

Setting from Orson & Blake Collectables.

1. Cut tops from pumpkins and discard tops. Scoop out seeds and membranes from pumpkins, leaving 1cm shells.

2. Heat oil in pan, add onion, garlic and ground spices, cook, stirring, until onions are soft. Add tomatoes and sugar, simmer, uncovered, about 10 minutes or until tomatoes are pulpy.

3. Combine tomato mixture with rice and beans; mix well. Spoon rice mixture into pumpkins. Place pumpkins in small baking dish. Bake, covered, in moderately hot oven about 1½ hours or until pumpkins are tender. Serve cut in half, sprinkled with fresh coriander. Serves 4.

■ Rice mixture can be made a day ahead.
■ Storage: Covered, in refrigerator.
■ Freeze: Not suitable.
■ Microwave: Suitable.

Cloth from Orson & Blake Collectables.

Stuffed Baby Pumpkins

You will need to cook ⅓ cup (65g) long-grain rice for this recipe.

2 x 450g small golden nugget pumpkins
1 tablespoon olive oil
1 medium (150g) onion, finely chopped
2 cloves garlic, crushed
2 teaspoons ground cumin
1 teaspoon ground coriander
2 teaspoons ground sweet paprika
1 teaspoon ground turmeric
3 medium (390g) tomatoes, finely chopped
1 teaspoon sugar
1 cup cooked white rice
¾ cup (110g) frozen broad beans, thawed, peeled
1 tablespoon chopped fresh coriander leaves

Tiles from Country Floors.

Cucumber with Minted Yogurt

4 small (500g) green cucumbers
2 cups (500ml) plain yogurt
¼ cup chopped fresh mint
1 clove garlic, crushed
½ teaspoon ground cumin
1 tablespoon lemon juice

1. Halve cucumbers lengthways, scoop out seeds. Finely chop cucumbers.

2. Combine cucumbers with remaining ingredients in bowl, cover; refrigerate at least 1 hour before serving.
Serves 4 to 6.

■ Recipe can be made 3 days ahead.
■ Storage: Covered, in refrigerator.
■ Freeze: Not suitable.

Olive, Tomato and Chilli Salad

4 medium (300g) egg tomatoes
1 small (100g) red Spanish onion
2½ cups (400g) seedless black olives
3 cups (150g) firmly packed
 watercress sprigs
1 bunch (120g) rocket
¼ cup (40g) drained bottled hot
 red chillies
1 tablespoon chopped fresh
 coriander leaves
DRESSING
2 tablespoons olive oil
1 tablespoon lemon juice
¼ teaspoon sugar
½ teaspoon chopped fresh
 rosemary
1 teaspoon cumin seeds
2 cloves garlic, crushed

1. Cut tomatoes into wedges. Slice onion, separate into rings.

2. Combine tomatoes, onion, olives, watercress, rocket and chillies in bowl; mix well. Drizzle with dressing; top with coriander.
Dressing: Combine all ingredients in jar; shake well.
Serves 6.

■ Recipe best made just
 before serving.
■ Freeze: Not suitable.

Bowl from Corso De' Fiori.

Vegetables in Coriander Sauce

2 tablespoons olive oil
250g celeriac, chopped
2 medium (300g) onions, sliced
3 cloves garlic, crushed
1 tablespoon ground cumin
2 teaspoons ground sweet paprika
1 teaspoon fennel seeds
½ teaspoon ground cinnamon
2 medium (400g) green peppers, chopped
250g baby yellow squash, halved
1 cup (250ml) tomato puree
2¼ cups (560ml) water
½ teaspoon sugar
½ cup chopped fresh coriander leaves

1. Heat oil in pan, add celeriac, onions and garlic, cook, stirring, about 10 minutes or until celeriac is tender.

2. Add spices, cook, stirring, until fragrant. Add peppers and squash.

3. Stir in combined puree and water, simmer, uncovered, stirring occasionally, about 15 minutes or until squash are tender and sauce has thickened. Stir in sugar and coriander.
Serves 4.

■ Recipe can be made a day ahead.
■ Storage: Covered, in refrigerator.
■ Freeze: Not suitable.
■ Microwave: Not suitable.

Honeyed Carrots with Sweet Potatoes

4 medium (480g) carrots
2 small (400g) sweet potatoes
50g butter, melted
1 tablespoon olive oil
1½ teaspoons ground cumin
1 teaspoon cumin seeds
¼ cup (60ml) honey
2 tablespoons chopped fresh parsley

1. Cut carrots into thick chunks. Cut sweet potatoes into thick slices.

2. Add carrots and sweet potatoes to pan of boiling water, simmer, uncovered, 5 minutes; drain.

3. Combine butter, oil, cumin, seeds and honey in bowl; mix well. Place vegetables on wire rack over baking dish. Brush vegetables with some butter mixture. Bake, uncovered, in hot oven about 20 minutes or until tender, brushing with remaining butter mixture throughout cooking. Serve sprinkled with parsley.
Serves 4.

■ Recipe best made just before serving.
■ Freeze: Not suitable.
■ Microwave: Not suitable.

2. Whisk oil and juice in small bowl until combined; add shallots and mint; mix well.

3. Combine half mint mixture with tomatoes in bowl; gently stir to combine. Combine remaining mint mixture with cheese in separate bowl; gently stir to combine. Refrigerate tomato mixture and cheese mixture, covered, at least 1 hour. Place cheese mixture on serving plate, sprinkle with half the topping, top with tomato mixture, then remaining topping.

4. Topping: Finely chop all ingredients. Serves 4 to 6.

- Tomato mixture, cheese mixture and topping can be made a day ahead.
- Storage: Covered, separately, in refrigerator.
- Freeze: Not suitable.

Yellow plate from House.

Tomato, Feta and Shallot Salad

4 medium (500g) tomatoes
500g feta cheese
1/3 cup (80ml) olive oil
1/4 cup (60ml) lemon juice
3 green shallots, finely chopped
2 tablespoons chopped fresh mint
TOPPING
2 tablespoons roughly chopped walnuts, toasted
3 teaspoons sesame seeds, toasted
1/4 teaspoon cumin seeds
1/4 teaspoon coriander seeds

1. Cut tomatoes into wedges, remove seeds and cores; chop tomatoes finely. Cut cheese into 1cm pieces.

Artichoke and Vegetable Salad

3 large (540g) carrots
1/3 cup (80ml) virgin olive oil
1 medium (150g) onion,
    finely chopped
1 teaspoon coriander seeds,
    crushed
2 teaspoons chopped fresh thyme
4 medium (800g) potatoes, quartered
1/2 cup (125ml) dry white wine
1 cup (250ml) water
1/2 medium cos lettuce, chopped
400g can artichoke hearts in brine,
    drained, quartered
1 tablespoon lemon juice
1 teaspoon cracked black pepper

1. Cut carrots into thick chunks.

2. Heat 1 tablespoon of the oil in pan, add onion, coriander and thyme, cook, stirring, until onion is soft.

3. Add carrots and potatoes to pan, cook, stirring, 5 minutes. Add remaining oil, wine and water, simmer, covered, about 10 minutes or until just tender. Stir in remaining ingredients.

Setting from Orson & Blake Collectables.

Serves 4 to 6.

▨ Recipe can be made a day ahead.
▨ Storage: Covered, in refrigerator.
▨ Freeze: Not suitable.
▨ Microwave: Suitable.

Minted Beetroot Salad

6 medium (1kg) fresh beetroot
1 cup (250ml) plain yogurt
1 clove garlic, chopped
1 tablespoon tahini
1½ tablespoons lemon juice
½ cup fresh mint leaves

1. Wash beetroot, trim leaves, leaving about 3cm of stem attached to beetroot. Add unpeeled beetroot to large pan of boiling water, boil, uncovered, about 45 minutes or until tender; drain.

2. Peel beetroot while warm; cut beetroot into wedges.

3. Blend or process remaining ingredients until mint is finely chopped. Serve beetroot topped with yogurt mixture. Serves 6 to 8.

■ Yogurt mixture can be made a day ahead.
■ Storage: Covered, in refrigerator.
■ Freeze: Not suitable.
■ Microwave: Beetroot suitable.

Beans with Walnut Tomato Sauce

1kg green beans
425g can tomatoes
1 tablespoon olive oil
2 cloves garlic, crushed
2 teaspoons ground cumin
2 teaspoons ground coriander
1/4 teaspoon cayenne pepper
3/4 cup (90g) chopped walnuts, toasted
1/2 cup chopped fresh coriander leaves
1 teaspoon sugar
1 small (150g) red pepper, thinly sliced
1 small (150g) yellow pepper, thinly sliced

1. Boil, steam or microwave beans until tender; drain.

2. Blend or process undrained tomatoes until smooth.

3. Heat oil in pan, add garlic, ground spices and nuts, cook, stirring, until fragrant. Add tomatoes, fresh coriander and sugar, cook, stirring, until heated through. Remove from heat, stir in peppers.

4. Combine beans with pepper mixture in large bowl; mix well.

Serves 6 to 8.

◼ Recipe best made close to serving.
◼ Freeze: Not suitable.
◼ Microwave: Suitable.

Layered Eggplant and Pepper Salad

3 medium (600g) red peppers
1kg (about 16) finger eggplants
1/3 cup (80ml) olive oil
**1/3 cup (50g) chopped pistachios,
    toasted**
YOGURT DRESSING
1 cup (250ml) plain yogurt
1 clove garlic, crushed
**1/4 cup chopped fresh
    coriander leaves**
**1 1/2 tablespoons chopped
    fresh oregano**
1 teaspoon ground cumin
2 teaspoons honey

1. Quarter peppers, remove seeds and membranes. Grill peppers, skin side up, until skin blisters and blackens. Peel away skin, slice peppers thickly.

2. Cut eggplants in halves lengthways. Heat 1 tablespoon of the oil in pan, add a third of the eggplants to pan, cook about 10 minutes, or until browned all over and very soft; drain on absorbent paper. Repeat with remaining oil and eggplants.

3. Spread quarter of the yogurt dressing onto serving plate; top with a third of the eggplants, then a third of the peppers. Repeat layering twice more. Top with remaining yogurt dressing; sprinkle with nuts.

4. Yogurt Dressing: Combine all ingredients in bowl; mix well.
Serves 6 to 8.

■ Peppers, eggplants and yogurt
    dressing can be prepared
    a day ahead.
■ Storage: Covered, separately,
    in refrigerator.
■ Freeze: Not suitable.
■ Microwave: Not suitable.

Dish and pot from Lucky Tom's; tassel and spoon from Morris Home & Garden Wares; rug from B.J. Homewares.

Breads, Grains & Pulses

Breads of many kinds are essential features of Middle Eastern cuisine, as are deliciously spiced staples such as couscous, burghul, chick peas, lentils, rice, and more.

Almond Coriander Couscous

3 cups (600g) couscous
3 cups (750ml) boiling water
1/4 cup (60ml) olive oil
1 clove garlic, crushed
2 green shallots, chopped
3/4 cup (105g) slivered almonds, toasted
1/3 cup (50g) dried currants
1/2 cup chopped fresh coriander leaves

2. Heat oil in large pan, add garlic and shallots, cook, stirring, until shallots are soft. Add couscous to pan, stir over heat until heated through.

1. Combine couscous and water in bowl, stand 5 minutes or until water is absorbed. Fluff couscous with fork.

3. Stir in nuts, currants and coriander. Serves 6.

▨ Recipe can be made 3 hours ahead.
▨ Storage: Covered, in refrigerator.
▨ Freeze: Not suitable.
▨ Microwave: Not suitable.

Bowl from Lucky Tom's; cutlery and tassel from Morris Home & Garden Wares.

Fruity Rice

50g ghee
1½ cups (300g) basmati rice
3 cups (750ml) water
250g fresh dates, seeded,
    thinly sliced
2 teaspoons orange flower water
½ cup (75g) dried apricots,
    thinly sliced
2 tablespoons chopped fresh parsley

1. Heat ghee in medium heavy-based pan, add rice, cook, stirring, until rice is coated with ghee. Add water, simmer, covered with tight-fitting lid, 12 minutes. Remove pan from heat, stand, covered, 10 minutes.

2. Stir in remaining ingredients. Serves 4 to 6.

▪ Recipe best made close to serving.
▪ Freeze: Not suitable.
▪ Microwave: Suitable.

Spicy Vegetables with Chick Peas

2 large (1kg) eggplants
coarse cooking salt
1/3 cup (80ml) olive oil
1 medium (350g) leek, chopped
2 cloves garlic, crushed
1 teaspoon ground cumin
1 teaspoon ground cardamom
1 teaspoon ground turmeric
1 teaspoon ground sweet paprika
1/2 teaspoon ground cinnamon
2 x 425g cans tomatoes
425g can chick peas, drained
3 small (270g) zucchini, sliced
150g green beans, halved
350g baby yellow squash, halved
200g baby carrots, halved
1/2 cup (75g) pistachios,
     toasted, chopped
1/3 cup chopped fresh parsley
1/4 cup chopped fresh mint
1/4 cup chopped fresh
     coriander leaves
1 1/2 cups (375ml) vegetable stock
1 bunch (500g) English spinach,
     shredded

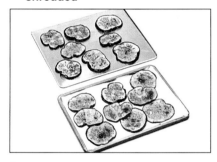

1. Cut eggplants into 1cm slices, place in colander, sprinkle with salt, stand 30 minutes. Rinse slices under cold water, drain, pat dry with absorbent paper. Brush slices with half the oil, place in single layer on trays, grill on both sides until lightly browned; drain on absorbent paper. Cut slices in half.

2. Heat remaining oil in pan, add leek, garlic and spices, cook, stirring, until leek is soft. Add undrained crushed tomatoes, chick peas, vegetables, nuts, herbs and stock, simmer, covered, until vegetables are tender.

3. Add spinach and eggplants to vegetable mixture, simmer, covered, about 5 minutes or until spinach is wilted. Serves 6.

■ Recipe can be made a day ahead.
■ Storage: Covered, in refrigerator.
■ Freeze: Not suitable.
■ Microwave: Suitable.

Spiced Fish with Chick Peas

4 (600g) firm white fish fillets
2 teaspoons ground turmeric
2 teaspoons ground cumin
1½ teaspoons ground cardamom
1½ tablespoons olive oil
1⅔ cups (410ml) chicken stock
2 x 300g cans chick peas,
    rinsed, drained
2 medium (400g) red peppers, sliced
¼ cup chopped fresh
    coriander leaves
1 tablespoon lemon juice

HERBED COUSCOUS
1½ cups (300g) couscous
1 teaspoon olive oil
1½ cups (375ml) boiling water
1 tablespoon chopped fresh
    coriander leaves

1. Coat fish in combined spices.

2. Heat oil in pan, add fish, cook until browned on both sides and tender. Remove fish from pan; keep warm. Discard oil.

3. Add stock, chick peas, peppers, coriander and juice to same pan, simmer, covered, about 10 minutes or until peppers are soft. Serve fish on herbed couscous with chick pea mixture.

4. **Herbed Couscous:** Place couscous in medium heatproof bowl, stir in oil, water and coriander; stand 5 minutes or until liquid is absorbed.
Serves 4.

■ Recipe best made just
  before serving.
■ Freeze: Not suitable.
■ Microwave: Not suitable.

Copper plate from Mr Brassman; basket from Orson & Blake Collectables.

Lavash

Poppy, caraway and sesame seeds can be used in this recipe. Sometimes this dough will become too elastic and difficult to roll; in this case, cover the dough, stand for 30 minutes then continue as directed.

1 teaspoon dried yeast
1 teaspoon honey
1 teaspoon sugar
1/2 cup (125ml) warm water
1 1/4 cups (185g) plain flour
2 teaspoons salt
1/4 teaspoon ground hot paprika
1/4 teaspoon cayenne pepper
1 egg white, lightly beaten
2 tablespoons seeds

2. Sift dry ingredients into large bowl. Stir in yeast mixture, mix to a firm dough. Knead dough on floured surface about 2 minutes or until dough is smooth. Place dough in oiled bowl, cover; refrigerate 45 minutes.

4. Prick rectangles with fork, brush lightly with egg white. Cut each rectangle into 16 triangles, sprinkle with seeds. Place triangles about 2cm apart on lightly floured oven trays. Bake in moderate oven about 10 minutes or until browned. Serve with hummus dip, if desired.
Makes 32.

▧ Recipe can be made a week ahead.
▧ Storage: In airtight container.
▧ Freeze: Not suitable.
▧ Microwave: Not suitable.

1. Combine yeast with honey and sugar in small bowl, stir in water, cover, stand in warm place about 15 minutes or until mixture is frothy.

3. Turn dough onto floured surface, knead until smooth. Divide dough in half, roll each half into a 13cm x 60cm rectangle.

Pita

1 tablespoon (14g) dried yeast
1 tablespoon honey
½ cup (125ml) warm water
3 cups (450g) white plain flour
1½ cups (240g) wholemeal
    plain flour
2 teaspoons salt
2 cups (500ml) water, extra
2 tablespoons olive oil

1. Combine yeast, honey and water in bowl, cover, stand in warm place about 10 minutes or until mixture is frothy.

2. Sift flours and salt into bowl; return husks to bowl. Stir in yeast mixture and extra water, mix to a soft dough.

3. Knead dough on floured surface about 10 minutes or until smooth and elastic. Place dough in oiled bowl, cover, stand in warm place about 1 hour or until doubled in size. Turn dough onto lightly floured surface, knead until smooth.

4. Divide dough into 12 pieces, roll each piece into a ball. Place balls on lightly floured tray, cover, stand in warm place about 30 minutes or until doubled in size.

5. Roll each ball into a 16cm round. Preheat a large frying pan, or an electric frypan on highest setting for 5 minutes, brush base of pan with oil. Place 1 round at a time into pan, cover, cook about 2 minutes on each side or until browned and cooked through. Repeat with remaining rounds, brushing pan each time with more oil.
Makes 12.

■ Recipe can be made a day ahead.
■ Storage: In airtight container.
■ Freeze: Cooked pita suitable.
■ Microwave: Not suitable.

Cloth and carved shutters from Anokhi.

Megadarra

1 cup (200g) brown lentils
2½ cups (625ml) water
½ cup (100g) white long-grain rice
3 cups (750ml) water, extra
1 teaspoon ground allspice
1 teaspoon ground coriander
1 teaspoon salt
1 teaspoon freshly ground
    black pepper
CARAMELISED ONIONS
¼ cup (60ml) olive oil
3 large (600g) onions, halved, sliced
3 teaspoons sugar
1 tablespoon balsamic vinegar
½ cup (125ml) water

1. Combine lentils and water in medium pan, simmer, uncovered, about 25 minutes or until just tender. Add rice, extra water, spices, salt, pepper and half the caramelised onions, cook, stirring, until mixture boils. Simmer, covered, stirring occasionally, about 15 minutes or until rice is tender. Serve warm or cold, topped with remaining caramelised onions.

2. Caramelised Onions: Heat oil in pan, add onions and sugar, cook, stirring, 5 minutes. Add vinegar and half the water, cook, stirring, 10 minutes. Add remaining water, cook about 5 minutes or until onions are caramelised. Serves 4.

■ Recipe can be made a day ahead.
■ Storage: Covered, in refrigerator.
■ Freeze: Not suitable.
■ Microwave: Not suitable.

Burghul Pilaf with Roasted Vegetables

3 medium (600g) red peppers
2 large (360g) parsnips
1/3 cup (80ml) olive oil
3 cloves garlic, crushed
6 cardamom pods, bruised
3 teaspoons ground cumin
1 teaspoon brown mustard seeds
1 teaspoon cumin seeds
1 teaspoon ground coriander
1 bunch (400g) baby carrots
4 small (360g) zucchini, halved
2 cups (320g) burghul
2½ cups (625ml) boiling
    chicken stock
BASIL DRESSING
1 cup (250ml) plain yogurt
1 cup firmly packed fresh
    basil leaves

Plate from The Essential Ingredient.

1. Cut peppers into 3cm strips. Cut parsnips into wedges.

2. Heat oil in large baking dish, add garlic and spices; stir over heat until fragrant. Add all vegetables, stir until coated with spice mixture. Bake, uncovered, in hot oven about 45 minutes, turning vegetables occasionally, or until vegetables are tender and lightly browned.

3. Place burghul in heatproof bowl, add stock, stand 30 minutes or until stock is absorbed. Serve roasted vegetables with burghul and basil dressing.

4. Basil Dressing: Blend or process yogurt and basil until chopped.
Serves 4 to 6.

■ Recipe best made close to serving.
■ Freeze: Not suitable.
■ Microwave: Not suitable.

Chick Peas with Spinach and Spices

2 tablespoons olive oil
1 medium (150g) onion, chopped
3 cloves garlic, crushed
1 teaspoon ground cinnamon
1 teaspoon ground sweet paprika
2 teaspoons ground coriander
2 teaspoons cumin seeds
3 x 425g cans chick peas,
    rinsed, drained
3 small (300g) tomatoes, chopped
2 tablespoons tomato paste
1/4 cup (40g) seedless chopped dates
1 cup (250ml) water
1/4 cup chopped fresh
    coriander leaves
2 tablespoons chopped fresh mint
1 bunch (500g) English spinach,
    chopped

1. Heat oil in pan, add onion, garlic and spices, cook, stirring, until onion is soft.

2. Stir in chick peas, tomatoes, paste and dates; then water and herbs, simmer, covered, about 10 minutes.

3. Stir in spinach, simmer, uncovered, about 5 minutes or until spinach is just wilted.
Serves 4 to 6.

■ Recipe can be made a day ahead.
■ Storage: Covered, in refrigerator.
■ Freeze: Not suitable.
■ Microwave: Suitable.

Pide

1 teaspoon dried yeast
2 cups (300g) plain flour
2 cups (500ml) warm water
3 cups (450g) plain flour, extra
2 teaspoons salt
⅓ cup (80ml) olive oil
2 tablespoons sesame seeds

1. Combine yeast and flour in bowl, gradually stir in water. Cover, stand in warm place about 30 minutes or until mixture is frothy.

2. Sift extra flour and salt into large bowl. Stir in yeast mixture and half the oil, mix to a soft dough. Knead dough on floured surface about 10 minutes or until dough is smooth and elastic. Place dough in oiled bowl, cover, stand in warm place about 1 hour or until doubled in size.

Coffee set from Lucky Tom's; bowl from The Essential Ingredient.

3. Divide dough into 8 portions. Roll each portion into a 12cm x 18cm oval. Place ovals on lightly floured trays, cover, stand in warm place 20 minutes. Roll into 14cm x 18cm ovals on floured surface.

4. Preheat oven tray in hot oven 5 minutes. Brush tray with some of the remaining oil, place 2 ovals on tray; make indents with fingertips. Brush with more of the oil; sprinkle with some of the seeds. Bake in hot oven about 8 minutes or until lightly browned. Repeat process with remaining ovals. Makes 8.

■ Recipe can be made a day ahead.
■ Storage: In airtight container.
■ Freeze: Cooked pide suitable.
■ Microwave: Not suitable.

Braised Chicken in Tomato Sauce

2 tablespoons olive oil
8 (880g) chicken thigh fillets, sliced
1 large (200g) onion, chopped
2 cloves garlic, finely sliced
1 teaspoon ground coriander
1/2 teaspoon ground turmeric
1/4 teaspoon cayenne pepper
4 medium (520g) tomatoes,
    peeled, chopped
3 cups (750ml) chicken stock
1 cinnamon stick
1 medium (200g) green pepper,
    sliced
200g baby yellow squash, quartered
2 (120g) finger eggplants,
    thickly sliced
1/2 cup (85g) raisins
1/4 cup (40g) blanched almonds,
    toasted
2 tablespoons chopped fresh
    coriander leaves
COUSCOUS
1 3/4 cups (430ml) water
20g butter, chopped
2 cups (400g) couscous

1. Heat oil in pan, add chicken in batches, cook until browned all over; remove from pan.

2. Add onion and garlic to same pan, cook, stirring, until onion is soft. Add ground spices, cook, stirring, until fragrant. Stir in tomatoes and stock.

3. Return chicken to pan with cinnamon stick, simmer, uncovered, about 30 minutes or until sauce has thickened slightly and chicken is tender, stirring occasionally. Add pepper, squash and eggplants, simmer, uncovered, about 5 minutes or until vegetables are tender. Discard cinnamon stick. Serve chicken mixture on couscous, top with raisins, nuts and fresh coriander.

4. Couscous: Bring water to boil in medium pan, stir in butter and couscous; remove from heat, cover, stand about 5 minutes or until water is absorbed. Serves 6.

▓ Recipe can be made 2 days ahead.
▓ Storage: Covered, in refrigerator.
▓ Freeze: Not suitable.
▓ Microwave: Not suitable.

Plates from Francalia, textured cloth from Accoutrement.

2. Sift semolina, flour and salt into large bowl, add yeast mixture, butter, rind, anise, extra water and egg, mix to a soft dough.

3. Knead dough on floured surface about 10 minutes or until smooth and elastic. Divide dough into 3 pieces, roll each piece into a ball. Place on greased oven tray; cover, stand in warm place about 1½ hours or until balls have doubled in size.

4. Flatten balls until 2cm thick, brush with egg yolk, sprinkle with seeds. Bake in moderate oven about 30 minutes or until bread is browned and sounds hollow when tapped. Cool on wire rack.
Makes 3.

- Recipe can be made a day ahead.
- Storage: In airtight container.
- Freeze: Suitable.
- Microwave: Not suitable.

Orange Anise Bread

2 teaspoons (7g) dried yeast
1 teaspoon sugar
2 tablespoons warm water
1½ cups (240g) semolina
1½ cups (225g) plain flour
1 teaspoon salt
90g butter, melted
1 tablespoon grated orange rind
2 teaspoons ground anise
2/3 cup (160ml) water, extra
1 egg, lightly beaten
1 egg yolk
1 tablespoon sesame seeds

1. Combine yeast, sugar and water in small bowl; cover, stand in warm place about 10 minutes or until frothy.

Brass plate and container from Mr Brassman.

Chicken Pilaf with Apricots

60g ghee
1kg chicken thigh fillets, chopped
2 medium (300g) onions, sliced
1 clove garlic, crushed
1 teaspoon ground cumin
1 teaspoon ground coriander
½ teaspoon ground turmeric
½ cup (75g) dried apricots, sliced
2 cups (400g) basmati rice
1 litre (4 cups) chicken stock
¼ cup (35g) dried currants
½ cup (60g) frozen peas
½ cup (80g) pine nuts, toasted

2. Heat remaining ghee in same pan, add onions, garlic and spices, cook, stirring, until onions are soft.

4. Remove from heat, stir in chicken, stand, covered, 15 minutes. Stir in currants, peas and nuts. Top with coriander, if desired.
Serves 6.

■ Recipe best made just before serving.
■ Freeze: Not suitable.
■ Microwave: Suitable.

1. Heat half the ghee in large pan, add chicken in batches, cook until lightly browned all over and tender; drain.

3. Add apricots and rice, stir over heat until rice is coated in spice mixture. Stir in stock, simmer, covered with tight-fitting lid, 15 minutes.

Chick Pea, Lentil and Bean Soup

1 tablespoon olive oil
1 large (300g) red Spanish onion,
    chopped
2 cloves garlic, crushed
1 teaspoon ground cumin
1 teaspoon ground turmeric
1 teaspoon ground sweet paprika
1/2 teaspoon ground cinnamon
2 x 425g cans chick peas,
    rinsed, drained
340g can red kidney beans,
    rinsed, drained
1/2 cup (100g) red lentils
1.25 litres (5 cups) vegetable stock
1/4 cup (60ml) lemon juice
1/3 cup chopped fresh mint
1 bunch (500g) English spinach,
    shredded

1. Heat oil in pan, add onion, garlic and spices, cook, stirring, until onion is soft.

2. Stir in peas, beans, lentils, stock, juice and mint, simmer, covered, about 20 minutes, stirring occasionally, or until lentils are tender.

3. Stir in spinach, simmer, uncovered, about 5 minutes or until spinach is just wilted.
Serves 6.

■ Recipe can be made a day ahead.
■ Storage: Covered, in refrigerator.
■ Freeze: Suitable.
■ Microwave: Suitable.

Braised Lamb and Eggplant with Pilaf

1 large (500g) eggplant
coarse cooking salt
2 tablespoons olive oil
1 large (300g) red Spanish onion,
   finely chopped
3 cloves garlic, crushed
600g chopped lean lamb
1/2 teaspoon ground cinnamon
1/4 teaspoon ground cardamom
1/2 teaspoon garam masala
1 teaspoon ground cumin
2 cups (500ml) water
2 cups (400g) basmati rice
3 cups (750ml) chicken stock
5 medium (600g) tomatoes,
   peeled, seeded, chopped
1 cup (150g) unsalted roasted
   cashews
1/4 cup chopped fresh
   coriander leaves

1. Cut eggplant into 1cm slices, place in colander, sprinkle with salt, stand 30 minutes. Rinse eggplant slices under cold water, drain on absorbent paper; chop eggplant.

2. Heat half the oil in large pan, add onion and garlic, cook, stirring, until onion is soft; remove from pan. Cut lamb into 2cm pieces. Heat remaining oil in same pan, add lamb, cook until browned all over, add spices, cook, stirring, until fragrant. Add onion mixture and water, simmer, covered, 45 minutes, stirring occasionally.

3. Add eggplant, simmer, covered, 45 minutes or until eggplant and lamb are tender.

4. Meanwhile, place rice in bowl, cover with hot water, stand until cool, rinse under cold water; drain.

5. Add stock to large heavy-based pan, bring to boil, add rice, simmer, covered with tight-fitting lid, 12 minutes. Remove from heat, stand 10 minutes. Stir in tomatoes, nuts and coriander. Serve pilaf topped with lamb and eggplant mixture. Serves 4 to 6.

▨ Recipe best made just
   before serving.
▨ Freeze: Not suitable.
▨ Microwave: Not suitable.

Bowl from Lucky Tom's; carpet and basket from Morris Home & Garden Wares.

Challah

1 tablespoon (14g) dried yeast
1 teaspoon sugar
½ cup (125ml) warm water
3 eggs
¼ cup (55g) sugar, extra
125g butter, melted
1½ cups (375ml) warm milk
1½ teaspoons salt
½ cup (80g) sultanas
6 cups (900g) plain flour
1 egg, lightly beaten, extra
1 tablespoon poppy seeds

1. Combine yeast with sugar in small bowl, stir in water, cover, stand in warm place about 10 minutes or until mixture is frothy.

2. Whisk eggs and extra sugar together in large bowl. Stir in yeast mixture, butter, milk, salt, sultanas and sifted flour in 2 batches; mix to a soft dough.

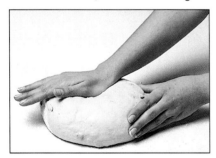

3. Knead dough on floured surface about 10 minutes or until dough is smooth and elastic.

4. Place dough in oiled bowl, cover, stand in warm place about 1 hour or until dough has doubled in size.

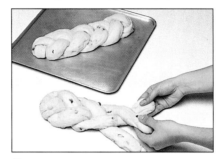

5. Divide dough into 6 pieces, roll each piece into a 40cm sausage. Plait 3 sausages together, place on greased oven tray. Repeat with remaining dough.

6. Cover dough, stand in warm place about 30 minutes or until almost doubled in size. Brush with extra egg, sprinkle with seeds. Bake in moderate oven about 30 minutes or until challah are browned and sound hollow when tapped. Cool on wire racks.
Makes 2.

■ Recipe best made on day of serving.
■ Freeze: Suitable.
■ Microwave: Not suitable.

Basket from B.J. Homewares; pot from Lucky Tom's.

Bowl from House.

1. Heat oil in large pan, add onions, garlic, ground spices and sambal oelek, cook over medium heat, stirring, until onions are soft.

2. Add paste, tomatoes, stock, lentils, sugar and coriander, simmer, uncovered, about 20 minutes or until lentils are tender. Serve topped with coriander yogurt.

3. Coriander Yogurt: Combine all ingredients in small bowl; mix well. Serves 6.

■ Soup and coriander yogurt can be made a day ahead.
■ Storage: Covered, separately, in refrigerator.
■ Freeze: Not suitable.
■ Microwave: Suitable.

Tomato, Lentil and Coriander Soup

1 tablespoon olive oil
2 medium (300g) onions, chopped
3 cloves garlic, crushed
1 teaspoon ground cumin
1/2 teaspoon garam masala
1/2 teaspoon sambal oelek
1/4 cup (60ml) tomato paste
12 medium (1.5kg) tomatoes, peeled, seeded, chopped
1.5 litres (6 cups) vegetable stock
1/2 cup (100g) red lentils
2 teaspoons sugar
1/3 cup chopped fresh coriander leaves

CORIANDER YOGURT
1 cup (250ml) plain yogurt
2 tablespoons chopped fresh parsley
2 tablespoons chopped fresh coriander leaves
1 teaspoon ground coriander

Serving bowl and vase from Lucky Tom's; under-plate and spoons from Morris Home & Garden Wares.

Vegetable Rice with Chick Peas

You will need to cook 1 cup (200g) long-grain rice for this recipe.

1 tablespoon olive oil
1 large (200g) onion, chopped
3 cloves garlic, crushed
1 teaspoon sambal oelek
2 teaspoons ground cumin
1/2 teaspoon ground cinnamon
1 teaspoon ground ginger
425g can tomatoes
150g baby yellow squash, quartered
2 tablespoons chopped fresh parsley
2 tablespoons chopped fresh coriander leaves
3 cups cooked white long-grain rice
2 x 425g cans chick peas, rinsed, drained
1/4 cup (60ml) orange juice

1. Heat oil in large pan, add onion, garlic, sambal oelek and spices, cook, stirring, until onions are soft.

2. Add undrained crushed tomatoes, squash and herbs, simmer, uncovered, until squash are tender.

3. Add rice, chick peas and juice, cook, stirring, until heated through.
Serves 6.

- Recipe best made just before serving.
- Freeze: Not suitable.
- Microwave: Suitable.

Khoubiz

2 teaspoons (7g) dried yeast
1 teaspoon sugar
1³/₄ cups (430ml) warm water
5 cups (750g) plain flour
1½ teaspoons salt
1 teaspoon ground cumin
2 tablespoons olive oil
½ cup (125ml) olive oil, extra
ONION CHEESE VARIATION
1 tablespoon olive oil
1 large (200g) onion, chopped
350g haloumi cheese, chopped
2 teaspoons za'atar seasoning
ZA'ATAR VARIATION
²/₃ cup (100g) za'atar seasoning
²/₃ cup (160ml) olive oil

1. Combine yeast, sugar and water in large bowl, gradually stir in half the sifted flour, cover, stand in warm place about 25 minutes or until frothy.

2. Stir in remaining sifted flour, salt, cumin and oil, mix to a firm dough. Knead dough on floured surface about 10 minutes or until smooth and elastic. Place dough in oiled bowl, cover, stand in warm place about 1 hour or until dough is almost doubled in size.

3. Turn dough onto floured surface, knead until smooth. Divide dough into 8 pieces, shape each piece into a ball. Roll each ball into a 20cm round; cover, stand 20 minutes to rest dough.

4. Brush base of heated pan lightly with some of the extra oil. Cook rounds of dough 1 at a time, covered, about 3 minutes or until lightly browned underneath. Turn bread over, cook, covered, about 2 minutes or until lightly browned on other side. Repeat with remaining oil and rounds of dough.

5. Onion Cheese Variation: Make khoubiz as directed to Step 3. Heat oil in pan, add onion, cook, stirring, until soft; cool. Sprinkle rounds of dough with combined onion mixture, cheese and seasoning; cook with onion side down, as directed in Step 4.

6. Za'atar Variation: Make khoubiz as directed to Step 3. Spread rounds of dough with combined seasoning and oil; cook with seasoning side down, as directed in Step 4.
Makes 8.

■ Recipe best made on day of serving.
■ Storage: In airtight container.
■ Freeze: Cooked khoubiz suitable.
■ Microwave: Not suitable.

Salad servers from B.J. Homewares; tray from Morris Home & Garden Wares; bowl from Lucky Tom's.

Saffron Orange Rice with Pine Nuts

2 tablespoons olive oil
1 clove garlic, crushed
1 large (200g) onion, chopped
1/4 teaspoon saffron threads
2 teaspoons grated orange rind
1/2 teaspoon ground cinnamon
1 teaspoon ground cumin
2 cups (400g) basmati rice
1 litre (4 cups) chicken stock
1/4 cup (35g) dried currants
2 tablespoons chopped fresh parsley
1/3 cup (50g) pine nuts, toasted

1. Heat oil in pan, add garlic and onion, cook, stirring, until onion is just soft. Add saffron, rind and spices.

2. Add rice, stir over heat until rice is coated with oil. Stir in stock, simmer, covered with tight-fitting lid, 12 minutes.

3. Remove from heat; stand, covered, 10 minutes. Stir in currants and parsley; sprinkle with nuts. Top with shredded orange rind, if desired. Serves 6.

■ Recipe best made just before serving.
■ Freeze: Not suitable.
■ Microwave: Not suitable.

Sweets & Drinks

The Middle Eastern ritual of serving coffee or mint tea with a mountain of sweets is well known throughout the world – these treats will whet your appetite for more than just baklava and Turkish delight.

Figs in Honey and Port Wine

We used corella pears in this recipe.

1 medium (140g) lemon
¼ cup (60ml) port
1½ cups (375ml) water
½ cup (125ml) honey
2 cinnamon sticks
1 vanilla bean, split
6 black peppercorns
8 medium (500g) fresh figs
2 medium (400g) pears, quartered
HONEYED MASCARPONE
2 egg yolks
2 tablespoons honey
250g mascarpone cheese
½ teaspoon ground nutmeg

2. Add figs and pears to pan, simmer, uncovered, about 5 minutes or until fruit is just tender. Remove fruit to bowl. Simmer syrup about 10 minutes or until thickened; pour over fruit. Serve fruit mixture at room temperature with honeyed mascarpone.

1. Peel rind thinly from lemon using a vegetable peeler. Cut any white pith from rind. Cut rind into very thin strips. Combine rind, port, water, honey, cinnamon sticks, vanilla bean and peppercorns in pan, boil, uncovered, about 10 minutes or until reduced by half.

3. Honeyed Mascarpone: Beat egg yolks and honey in small bowl with electric mixer until thick and pale, stir in mascarpone and nutmeg.
Serves 4 to 6.

■ Recipe can be made a day ahead.
■ Storage: Fruit mixture and honeyed mascarpone, covered, separately, in refrigerator.
■ Freeze: Not suitable.
■ Microwave: Not suitable.

Footed bowl from Home & Garden on the Mall.

China from Lucky Tom's.

Date and Nut Crescents

1²/₃ cups (250g) plain flour
125g butter, chopped
¹/₄ cup (60ml) iced water, approximately
icing sugar mixture
FILLING
250g (about 10) fresh dates, seeded, chopped
¹/₃ cup (80ml) water
³/₄ cup (75g) walnuts, toasted, chopped
¹/₄ teaspoon ground cinnamon

1. Sift flour into large bowl, rub in butter, gradually stir in enough water to mix to a firm dough. Knead dough on lightly floured surface about 5 minutes or until smooth, cover; refrigerate 1 hour.

2. Roll pastry on floured surface until 3mm thick, cut into 7cm rounds.

3. Brush edges of rounds with water, drop a teaspoon of filling into centre of each round, fold over to enclose filling; press edges together. Shape into crescents, place 2cm apart on greased oven trays. Bake in a moderate oven about 20 minutes; cool on wire racks. Toss crescents in sifted icing sugar.

4. Filling: Combine dates and water in small pan, simmer, uncovered, about 5 minutes or until dates are softened. Stir in remaining ingredients; cool. Makes about 40.

- Recipe can be made 2 days ahead.
- Storage: In airtight container.
- Freeze: Not suitable.
- Microwave: Not suitable.

Semolina Cake

125g butter
1 teaspoon vanilla essence
¾ cup (150g) firmly packed
 brown sugar
2 eggs
2 cups (320g) semolina
1 teaspoon baking powder
½ teaspoon bicarbonate of soda
¾ cup (180ml) low-fat sour cream
⅓ cup (50g) roasted hazelnuts
SYRUP
1½ cups (330g) caster sugar
1 cup (250ml) water
2 tablespoons lemon juice

4. Syrup: Combine sugar and water in medium pan, stir over low heat, without boiling, until sugar is dissolved. Stir in juice, simmer, uncovered, without stirring, about 7 minutes or until slightly thickened (do not allow syrup to change colour).

- Recipe can be made a day ahead.
- Storage: In airtight container.
- Freeze: Suitable.
- Microwave: Not suitable.

1. Beat butter, essence and sugar in small bowl with electric mixer until light and fluffy. Add eggs 1 at a time, beating well between additions.

2. Stir in combined sifted semolina, baking powder and soda alternately with sour cream.

3. Spread mixture evenly into greased 20cm x 30cm lamington pan; top with nuts. Bake in moderate oven about 30 minutes. Pour hot syrup over hot cake in pan; cool in pan.

Tiles from Country Floors.

Sesame Honey Fritters

2 teaspoons (7g) dried yeast
1 teaspoon sugar
1/3 cup (80ml) warm water
3/4 cup (110g) plain flour
1/2 teaspoon salt
3/4 cup (110g) sesame seeds, toasted
1 1/4 cups (185g) plain flour, extra
1/4 cup (60ml) vegetable oil
2 tablespoons white wine vinegar
1 tablespoon orange flower water
1 egg yolk
50g butter, melted
vegetable oil for deep-frying
2 cups (500ml) honey
1/4 cup (35g) sesame seeds,
  toasted, extra

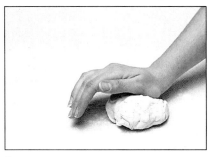

1. Combine yeast, sugar and water in small bowl, cover; stand in warm place about 10 minutes or until frothy.

2. Sift flour and salt into medium bowl, add yeast mixture, mix to a firm dough. Knead dough on floured surface about 10 minutes or until smooth and elastic. Place dough in oiled bowl, cover, stand in warm place about 1 1/2 hours or until dough has doubled in size.

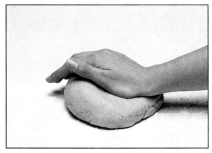

3. Blend or process seeds until finely crushed, place in large bowl with extra sifted flour, oil, vinegar, orange flower water, egg yolk and butter; mix well.

4. Add sesame mixture to yeast mixture, mix to a soft dough. Knead dough on floured surface about 10 minutes or until smooth and elastic.

Tiles from Country Floors; wooden tray from Morris Home & Garden Wares.

5. Roll tablespoons of dough into 16cm sausages, cut each in half. Press 2 ends together, twist shapes, press ends together; repeat with remaining dough. Place twists on trays, cover, stand in warm place about 30 minutes or until nearly doubled in size.

6. Deep-fry fritters in hot oil in batches a few minutes or until browned all over; drain on absorbent paper.

7. Add honey to medium heatproof bowl, place bowl over pan of simmering water. Place hot fritters in warm honey in batches; stand 5 minutes. Drain on wire rack over tray, sprinkle with extra seeds. Serve cold.
Makes about 30.

■ Recipe can be made 3 hours ahead.
■ Storage: Covered, in refrigerator.
■ Freeze: Not suitable.
■ Microwave: Not suitable.

Tiles from Country Floors.

Honeyed Strawberry Smoothie

2 cups (500ml) milk
6 strawberries, hulled
2 tablespoons honey
1 tablespoon lemon juice
6 ice cubes

1. Blend or process all ingredients until smooth.
Makes about 2½ cups (625ml).

■ Recipe best made just before serving.
■ Freeze: Not suitable.

Pear and Cashew Pudding

3 sheets ready-rolled puff pastry
1¼ cups (185g) chopped
    dried pears
½ cup (80g) sultanas
1 cup (150g) unsalted roasted
    cashews, finely chopped
1 teaspoon grated lemon rind
400g can sweetened condensed
    milk
2¼ cups (560ml) milk
¼ cup (50g) brown sugar
½ teaspoon ground cinnamon
½ teaspoon ground cardamom
2 eggs, lightly beaten

1. Place pastry sheets on 3 lightly greased oven trays. Bake in moderately hot oven about 10 minutes or until browned and puffed.

2. Crumble 1 sheet of pastry evenly into greased ovenproof dish (4 litre/16 cup capacity). Sprinkle with half the pears, half the sultanas and a third of the nuts; repeat layering process. Top with remaining pastry and nuts.

3. Whisk rind, milks, sugar, spices and eggs together in large jug, pour into dish. Bake in moderately slow oven about 30 minutes or until top is browned and pudding set.
Serves 8.

■ Recipe best made just before serving.
■ Freeze: Not suitable.
■ Microwave: Not suitable.

Creamed Honey Rice

1.5 litres (6 cups) milk
¼ cup (60ml) honey
¾ cup (150g) white short-grain rice
¼ cup (35g) dried currants
1 teaspoon ground cardamom
**1 tablespoon chopped unsalted
    cashews, toasted**
**1 tablespoon chopped pistachios,
    toasted**

1. Combine milk and honey in large pan, stir over heat until honey is melted; bring to boil.

2. Add rice, currants and cardamom to pan, simmer, uncovered, about 45 minutes or until rice is tender and mixture thick, stirring occasionally. Serve warm, topped with nuts. Drizzle with cream and extra honey, if desired. Serves 4 to 6.

■ Recipe best made just
   before serving.
■ Freeze: Not suitable.
■ Microwave: Suitable.

China from Corso De' Fiori.

Sesame Seed Brittle

1½ cups (330g) sugar
¼ cup (60ml) water
½ cup (125ml) honey
2 cups (300g) sesame seeds

1. Grease 26cm x 32cm Swiss roll pan, cover base with baking paper. Combine sugar, water and honey in medium pan, stir over heat, without boiling, until sugar is dissolved. Brush sugar crystals from side of pan with brush dipped in water.

4. Allow bubbles to subside, pour mixture into prepared pan. Stand 10 minutes, mark into desired shapes. When cold, break into pieces.

■ Recipe can be made 3 days ahead.
■ Storage: In airtight container.
■ Freeze: Not suitable.
■ Microwave: Not suitable.

2. Boil, uncovered, without stirring, until mixture reaches soft ball stage (116°C) on candy thermometer (a teaspoon of mixture will form a soft ball when dropped into a cup of cold water).

3. Allow bubbles to subside, gently stir in seeds. Return mixture to boil, simmer, without stirring, until mixture reaches small crack stage (138°C) on candy thermometer (syrup forms a fine thread when dropped into cold water and can be snapped with the fingers).

Coffee cups and saucers from Opus; tiles from Country Floors.

Helva

1 cup (250ml) water
1 cup (250ml) milk
1 cup (220g) sugar
125g butter
3/4 cup (120g) semolina
1/2 cup (80g) blanched almonds,
  finely chopped
1 teaspoon ground cinnamon

1. Combine water, milk and sugar in medium pan, stir over heat, without boiling, until sugar is dissolved. Simmer, uncovered, without stirring, about 10 minutes or until slightly thickened.

2. Meanwhile, heat butter in medium pan, add semolina and nuts, cook, stirring constantly, about 5 minutes or until semolina is lightly browned; remove from heat.

3. Gradually stir hot milk mixture into semolina mixture, add cinnamon, stir over heat until boiling, reduce heat, cook, stirring, 1 minute. Remove from heat, cover pan with greaseproof paper, then lid; stand 15 minutes.

4. Grease 20cm x 30cm lamington pan, cover base and 2 opposite sides with sheet of baking paper. Spread mixture evenly into pan, stand 10 minutes. Turn helva onto board, cut into squares to serve. Dust with extra cinnamon, if desired.

▇ Recipe can be made 2 days ahead.
▇ Storage: Covered, in refrigerator.
▇ Freeze: Not suitable.
▇ Microwave: Not suitable.

Lime Pistachio Sherbet

1 cup (220g) sugar
2½ cups (625ml) water
2 teaspoons finely grated lime rind
1¼ cups (310ml) lime juice
¼ cup (35g) pistachios,
    finely chopped
2 egg whites
green food colouring

1. Combine sugar and water in medium pan, stir over heat, without boiling, until sugar is dissolved. Simmer, uncovered, without stirring, about 10 minutes or until mixture is slightly thickened; cool.

2. Stir in rind, juice and nuts, pour into lamington pan, cover with foil; freeze until firm.

3. Chop sherbet, place in large bowl with egg whites and a little colouring, beat with electric mixer until smooth. Return mixture to lamington pan, cover with foil, freeze until firm.

4. Chop sherbet, beat in large bowl with electric mixer until smooth. Return mixture to pan, cover with foil, freeze until firm.
Serves 4 to 6.

■ Recipe can be made 3 days ahead.
■ Storage: In freezer.
■ Microwave: Not suitable.

Orange Almond Cookies

200g butter, chopped
1 tablespoon finely grated
    orange rind
1 cup (160g) icing sugar mixture
2 teaspoons orange flower water
2 eggs, lightly beaten
2 cups (300g) plain flour
2½ cups (310g) packaged
    ground almonds
¼ cup (40g) blanched almonds,
    halved

1. Beat butter, rind, sifted icing sugar and orange flower water in small bowl with electric mixer until light and fluffy. Add eggs gradually, beat until just combined. Transfer mixture to large bowl. Stir in sifted flour and ground nuts, mix to a soft dough. Wrap dough in plastic, refrigerate 30 minutes.

2. Roll tablespoons of mixture into balls. Place balls about 4cm apart on greased oven trays, flatten slightly, press halved nuts into centres. Bake cookies in moderate oven about 15 minutes or until lightly browned. Cool cookies on trays.
Makes about 45.

■ Recipe can be made a week ahead.
■ Storage: In airtight container.
■ Freeze: Suitable.
■ Microwave: Not suitable.

Spiced Milk Tea

1 star anise
2 cloves
1 cardamom pod
2 coriander seeds
1 teaspoon ground ginger
1 cinnamon stick, halved
2 jasmine tea bags
½ cup (110g) caster sugar
1 litre (4 cups) water
3 cups (750ml) milk
¼ cup (20g) flaked almonds,
    toasted, crushed

1. Using mortar and pestle, lightly crush star anise, cloves, cardamom and coriander.

2. Combine anise mixture, ginger, cinnamon, tea bags, sugar, water and milk in large pan, stir over heat, without boiling, until sugar dissolves; bring to boil. Strain mixture into jug; serve warm topped with nuts.
Makes about 1.75 litres (7 cups).

■ Recipe best made just
    before serving.
■ Freeze: Not suitable.
■ Microwave: Suitable.

2. Grease large shallow ovenproof dish (4 litre/16 cup capacity), line with baking paper. Place half the pastry mixture over base of prepared dish. Spread combined remaining ingredients over pastry.

3. Top with remaining pastry. Bake in moderate oven about 30 minutes or until browned. Pour hot syrup immediately over pastry, cool. Cover, refrigerate 3 hours or overnight.

Plate from Country Floors.

4. Syrup: Combine all ingredients in medium pan, stir over heat, without boiling, until sugar is dissolved. Simmer, uncovered, without stirring, about 15 minutes or until mixture is slightly thickened.

■ Recipe best made a day ahead.
■ Storage: Covered, in refrigerator.
■ Freeze: Not suitable.
■ Microwave: Not suitable.

Konafa

375g packet kataifi shredded pastry
185g butter, melted
2 cups (400g) ricotta cheese
½ cup (60g) chopped pecans
1 cup (150g) dried apricots,
    chopped
½ teaspoon ground nutmeg
½ teaspoon ground ginger
½ cup (125ml) plain yogurt
2 tablespoons maple-flavoured
    syrup
SYRUP
1½ cups (375ml) water
1¾ cups (385g) sugar
¼ cup (60ml) maple-flavoured syrup
1 tablespoon orange flower water

1. Place pastry in large bowl, pull strands of pastry apart, pour butter over pastry, mix well.

Gold-rimmed Moroccan box from The Pacific East India Co.

Orange Coconut Cake

We used a sauternes in this recipe.

250g butter, chopped
1 tablespoon grated orange rind
¼ cup (55g) caster sugar
4 eggs
1 cup (150g) self-raising flour
¼ teaspoon baking powder
2 teaspoons ground cinnamon
1 cup (125g) packaged ground almonds
1½ cups (135g) coconut
½ cup (60g) chopped pecans
½ cup (125ml) orange juice
¼ cup (60ml) sweet white wine
¼ cup (20g) flaked almonds
SYRUP
1 cup (220g) caster sugar
⅔ cup (160ml) orange juice

1. Grease deep 23cm round cake pan, line pan with baking paper. Beat butter, rind and sugar in small bowl with electric mixer until light and fluffy. Add eggs 1 at a time, beating well between additions.

2. Transfer mixture to large bowl. Stir in sifted flour, baking powder and cinnamon, ground almonds, coconut and pecans. Stir in juice and wine.

3. Spread mixture into prepared pan, sprinkle with flaked almonds. Bake in moderate oven about 45 minutes. Pour hot syrup over hot cake in pan. Cool in pan.

4. Syrup: Combine sugar and juice in pan, stir over low heat, without boiling, until sugar is dissolved, boil, uncovered, without stirring, about 5 minutes or until syrup is slightly thickened.

■ Recipe can be made a day ahead.
■ Storage: In airtight container.
■ Freeze: Suitable.
■ Microwave: Not suitable.

Baked Spiced Quinces

6 medium (2kg) quinces
1 medium (180g) orange
1 litre (4 cups) boiling water
2 cups (440g) caster sugar
2 vanilla beans, split
4 cardamom pods, crushed
1 cinnamon stick
1 tablespoon honey
½ cup (125ml) orange juice

1. Peel and halve quinces, cut each half into 4 pieces; remove core.

2. Peel 4 thin strips of rind from orange using a vegetable peeler. Cut strips of rind into very thin strips.

3. Combine boiling water and sugar in jug, stir until sugar is dissolved. Place quinces in large shallow ovenproof dish (4.5 litre/18 cup capacity). Add rind, vanilla beans, cardamom and cinnamon. Pour sugar syrup over quinces.

4. Bake quinces, covered, in moderately hot oven about 2 hours or until quinces are changed in colour, tender and liquid is syrupy. Carefully remove quinces to large bowl. Stir honey and juice into syrup mixture in dish; pour over quinces in bowl, cover; refrigerate 3 hours or overnight. Remove cinnamon and vanilla beans.
Serves 6 to 8.

▓ Recipe can be made 3 days ahead.
▓ Storage: Covered, in refrigerator.
▓ Freeze: Not suitable.
▓ Microwave: Not suitable.

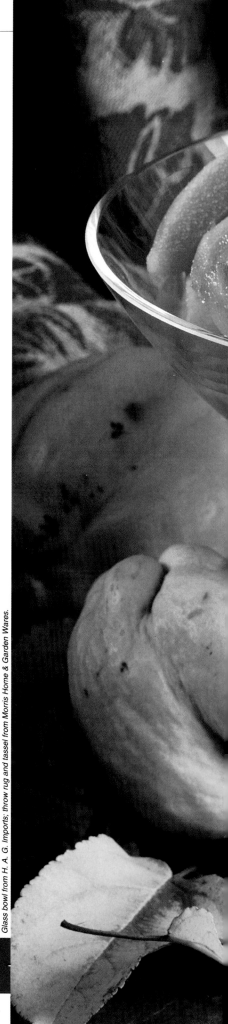

Glass bowl from H. A. G. Imports; throw rug and tassel from Morris Home & Garden Wares.

Baklava

1½ cups (165g) packaged ground hazelnuts
1 cup (125g) finely chopped hazelnuts
⅓ cup (75g) caster sugar
1 teaspoon ground cinnamon
180g ghee, melted
12 sheets fillo pastry
ORANGE SYRUP
1 cup (220g) caster sugar
⅔ cup (160ml) water
1 teaspoon grated orange rind
½ teaspoon ground cinnamon

Tiles from Country Floors.

1. Combine all the nuts, sugar and cinnamon in bowl.

2. Grease 20cm x 30cm lamington pan with a little of the ghee. Layer 3 pastry sheets together, brushing each with a little more ghee. Fold layered sheets in half, press into pan.

3. Sprinkle with one-third of nut mixture. Continue layering with remaining pastry, more ghee and nut mixture, ending with pastry. Trim pastry edge to fit pan.

Almond Milk

¼ cup (40g) blanched almonds, toasted
¾ cup (180ml) plain yogurt
2 cups (500ml) milk
½ teaspoon ground cinnamon
2 tablespoons caster sugar
6 ice cubes

1. Blend or process nuts until finely chopped.

2. Add remaining ingredients, blend or process until smooth.
Makes about 3 cups (750ml).

■ Recipe best made just before serving.
■ Freeze: Not suitable.

■ Baklava can be made
a week ahead.
■ Storage: In airtight container.
■ Freeze: Not suitable.
■ Microwave: Not suitable.

4. Cut 5 strips lengthways through layered pastry, cut each strip into 5 diamonds. Pour over any remaining ghee. Bake in moderate oven 30 minutes, reduce heat to slow, bake about 10 minutes or until browned. Pour hot syrup over hot baklava; cool in pan.

5. Orange Syrup: Combine all ingredients in medium pan; stir over low heat, without boiling, until sugar is dissolved. Simmer, uncovered, without stirring, about 5 minutes or until syrupy.

Turkish Delight

4 cups (880g) caster sugar
1 litre (4 cups) water
1 teaspoon lemon juice
1 cup (150g) cornflour
1 teaspoon cream of tartar
1½ tablespoons rosewater
red food colouring
¾ cup (120g) pure icing sugar
¼ cup (35g) cornflour, extra

1. Combine sugar, 1½ cups (375ml) of the water and juice in medium pan, stir over low heat, without boiling, until sugar is dissolved. Brush sugar crystals from side of pan with brush dipped in water. Simmer, uncovered, without stirring, until mixture reaches soft ball stage (116°C) on candy thermometer (a teaspoon of mixture will form a soft ball when dropped into a cup of cold water). Remove from heat.

2. Meanwhile, in separate medium heavy-based pan, blend cornflour and cream of tartar with enough of the remaining water to make a smooth paste. Stir in remaining water, whisk constantly over heat until mixture boils and thickens.

Plate from Country Floors

3. Gradually pour hot syrup in a thin stream into cornflour mixture, whisking constantly. Simmer gently, uncovered, about 1 hour or until mixture is translucent and a pale straw colour; stir occasionally during cooking.

4. Stir in rosewater, tint with colouring. Pour and spread mixture into greased deep 19cm square cake pan, stand, uncovered, 3 hours or overnight. Cut jelly into squares using oiled knife.

5. Coat squares in combined sifted icing sugar and extra cornflour.

■ Recipe can be made a day ahead.
■ Storage: In airtight container.
■ Freeze: Not suitable.
■ Microwave: Not suitable.

Iced Mint Tea

**1½ cups firmly packed fresh
  mint leaves**
3 Chinese green tea bags
2 tablespoons sugar
3 cups (750ml) boiling water

1. Combine mint, tea bags, sugar and water in large heatproof bowl, stand 15 minutes.

2. Strain mixture into jug; cool to room temperature. Refrigerate.
Makes about 3 cups (750ml).

■ Recipe can be made a day ahead.
■ Storage: Covered, in refrigerator.
■ Freeze: Not suitable.

Poppy Seed Cookies

200g butter, chopped
2 teaspoons grated lime rind
1/3 cup (75g) caster sugar
1/2 teaspoon ground cinnamon
2 teaspoons lime juice
1 tablespoon poppy seeds
1 3/4 cups (260g) plain flour
1/4 cup (35g) macadamia nuts,
    quartered

1. Beat butter, rind, sugar and cinnamon in small bowl with electric mixer until just combined. Stir in juice and seeds, then sifted flour in 2 batches.

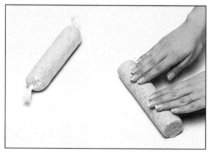

2. Divide mixture in half, roll each piece on floured surface to an 18cm sausage. Wrap in plastic, refrigerate until firm. Trim ends, cut into 8mm slices.

3. Place cookies about 2cm apart on greased oven trays; press nuts into centres. Bake in moderate oven about 12 minutes or until lightly browned. Stand 5 minutes, cool on wire racks. Makes about 48.

- Cookies can be made 3 days ahead.
- Storage: In airtight container.
- Freeze: Suitable.
- Microwave: Not suitable.

Platter from Waterford Wedgwood.

Cake stand from The Essential Ingredient; cake slice from Morris Home

Honey Yogurt Cake

200g unsalted butter, chopped
3/4 cup (180ml) plain yogurt
1/2 teaspoon ground cinnamon
1/2 cup (125ml) honey
2 eggs
1/4 cup (55g) caster sugar
1 3/4 cups (260g) self-raising flour
1/2 teaspoon baking powder
1 tablespoon icing sugar mixture
1/2 teaspoon ground cinnamon, extra

1. Grease 15cm x 25cm loaf pan, line base with baking paper. Beat butter, yogurt, cinnamon and honey in small bowl with electric mixer until just combined and smooth. Transfer mixture to large bowl.

2. Beat eggs and sugar in small bowl with electric mixer until thick and creamy.

3. Stir egg mixture into yogurt mixture. Fold in sifted flour and baking powder.

4. Spread mixture into prepared pan. Bake in moderate oven about 45 minutes. Stand cake 10 minutes before turning onto wire rack to cool. Serve dusted with combined sifted icing sugar and extra cinnamon.

■ Recipe can be made a day ahead.
■ Storage: In airtight container.
■ Freeze: Suitable.
■ Microwave: Not suitable.

Almond Cream with Spiced Fruit

¼ cup (35g) rice flour
¼ cup (55g) caster sugar
3 cups (750ml) milk
½ teaspoon grated lemon rind
¾ cup (90g) packaged
    ground almonds
¼ cup (35g) slivered almonds
1 tablespoon rosewater

SPICED FRUIT
½ cup (45g) dried apples
¾ cup (110g) dried apricots
½ cup (85g) seedless prunes
1 litre (4 cups) water
¾ cup (165g) caster sugar
2 cinnamon sticks
3 cloves
2 teaspoons Amaretto
1 tablespoon rosewater
¼ cup (30g) chopped walnuts

Bowl from B. J. Homewares.

1. Blend rice flour and sugar with ½ cup (125ml) of the milk in small bowl. Bring remaining milk and rind to boil in medium pan, stir in flour mixture, stir constantly over heat until mixture boils and thickens.

2. Stir in remaining ingredients. Spoon mixture into 6 dishes (¾ cup/180ml capacity); cool. Cover, refrigerate until cold. Serve with spiced fruit.

3. Spiced Fruit: Place fruit in bowl, cover with water; stand 2 hours. Drain fruit, discard water. Bring measured water, sugar, cinnamon, cloves, liqueur and rosewater to boil in medium pan, simmer, uncovered, about 30 minutes or until mixture is syrupy and reduced to about 2½ cups (625ml). Remove from heat, stir in fruit and nuts, cool. Cover; refrigerate 3 hours or overnight. Serves 6.

■ Recipe can be made 2 days ahead.
■ Storage: Covered, separately, in refrigerator.
■ Freeze: Not suitable.
■ Microwave: Suitable.

Cardamom Coffee

3 cardamom pods
2 tablespoons coarsely ground dark
   roasted coffee beans
1 teaspoon sugar
1 cup (250ml) water

1. Place cardamom pods on oven tray. Toast in moderate oven about 4 minutes; cool. Using mortar and pestle, lightly crush pods.

2. Combine cardamom, coffee, sugar and water in small pan, stir over heat until mixture comes up to boiling point; remove from heat.

3. Stand a minute or 2 to allow coffee grains to settle. Strain into tiny coffee cups to serve.
Serves 4.

▨ Recipe best made just before serving.
▨ Freeze: Not suitable.
▨ Microwave: Suitable.

Almond Date Spirals

**5 sheets fillo pastry
40g butter, melted
400g seedless fresh dates, chopped
½ teaspoon ground cinnamon
½ teaspoon ground nutmeg
½ teaspoon ground ginger
½ cup (125ml) cream
½ cup (40g) flaked almonds, toasted
2 teaspoons grated lemon rind**

1. Trim a sheet of baking paper to same size as a sheet of pastry, place on bench. Layer sheets of pastry together on paper, brushing each layer of pastry with a little of the butter.

2. Combine dates, spices, cream, nuts and rind in medium pan, cook, stirring, until dates are soft and almost all the cream is absorbed; cool.

3. Spread date mixture over pastry, leaving 4cm border at 1 long side. Roll pastry from other long side, using paper as a guide. Cover; refrigerate 30 minutes. Cut roll into 1.5cm slices, place cut side up, about 2cm apart on greased oven tray. Bake in moderate oven about 20 minutes or until pastry is crisp. Makes about 25.

China from Waterford Wedgwood.

■ Recipe best made on day of serving.
■ Storage: In airtight container in refrigerator.
■ Freeze: Not suitable.
■ Microwave: Not suitable.

Glossary

Parsley

Dill

Vanilla bean

Flat-leaf parsley

Star anise

Rosemary

Here are some terms, names and alternatives to help everyone use and understand our recipes perfectly.

ALLSPICE: pimento.

ALMONDS:
Blanched: nuts with skin removed.
Flaked: sliced nuts.
Ground: we used packaged commercially ground nuts.
Slivered: nuts cut lengthways.

AMARETTO: an almond-flavoured liqueur.

BAKING POWDER: a raising agent consisting of a starch, but mostly cream of tartar and bicarbonate of soda in the proportions of 1 level teaspoon of cream of tartar to 1/2 level teaspoon of bicarbonate of soda. This is equivalent to 2 teaspoons of baking powder.

BEEF:
Chuck steak: from neck area.
Minced: ground beef.

BICARBONATE OF SODA: baking soda.

BURGHUL (cracked wheat): wheat that is steamed until partly cooked, cracked then dried. Cracked wheat can be substituted.

BUTTER: use salted or unsalted (sweet) butter; 125g is equal to 1 stick butter.

BUTTERMILK: is now made by adding a culture to a low-fat milk to give a slightly acidic flavour; a low-fat milk can be substituted, if preferred.

CAJUN SEASONING: a combination of dried ingredients consisting of salt, blended peppers, garlic, onion and spices.

CELERIAC: tuberous root with brown skin, white flesh and a celery-like flavour.

CHEESE:
Cream: also known as Philly.
Feta: a soft Greek cheese with a sharp, salty taste.
Haloumi: a firm, cream-coloured sheep's milk cheese. A little like feta in flavour.
Kefalograviera: a semi-hard cheese with a smooth texture and a slightly salty aftertaste; made from sheep's milk.
Mascarpone: a fresh, unripened smooth triple cream cheese with a rich, sweet taste, slightly acidic.
Ricotta: a fresh, unripened light curd cheese.
Tasty cheddar: matured cheddar; use a hard, good-tasting variety.

CHICK PEAS: also known as ceci and garbanzos; 1/2 cup (100g) dried chick peas equals a 300g can of chick peas. Soak dried peas overnight in cold water, drain. Add to pan of water, bring to boil, simmer, covered, 1 hour or until tender.

CHILLIES: available in many different types and sizes. Use rubber gloves when chopping fresh chillies as they can burn your skin.
Bottled hot red: whole small red chillies in a vinegar and salt solution.
Dried crushed: available from supermarkets and Asian food stores.
Powder: the Asian variety is the hottest, made from ground chillies; it can be used as a substitute for fresh chillies in the proportions of 1/2 teaspoon chilli powder to 1 medium chopped fresh chilli.

COCONUT: use desiccated coconut unless otherwise specified.

COLOURINGS: we used concentrated liquid vegetable food colourings.

CORELLA PEAR: miniature dessert pear up to 10cm long.

CORNFLOUR: cornstarch.

COUSCOUS: a fine cereal made from semolina.

CREAM: fresh pouring cream; has a minimum fat content of 35%.
Low fat sour: a less dense, commercially cultured soured cream; this cream will not set as firmly as sour cream. It contains 18% milk fat.
Thickened (whipping): has a minimum fat content of 35%, plus a thickener.

CREAM OF TARTAR: an ingredient in baking powder. It is also sometimes added to confectionery mixtures to help prevent sugar from crystallising.

EGGPLANT: aubergine.

ENGLISH SPINACH: a soft-leaved vegetable, more delicate in taste than silverbeet; young silverbeet can be substituted for English spinach.

FILLO PASTRY: also known as phyllo dough; comes in tissue-thin pastry sheets bought chilled or frozen.

FLOUR:
Rice: flour made from ground rice.
Soya: flour made from ground soya beans.
White plain: all-purpose flour.
Wholemeal plain: wholewheat flour without the addition of baking powder.

GARAM MASALA: a combination of powdered spices, consisting of cardamom, cinnamon, cloves, coriander, cumin and nutmeg in varying proportions. Sometimes pepper is used to make a hot variation.

GHEE: a pure butter fat available in cans, it can be heated to high temperatures without burning because of the lack of salts and milk solids.

GHERKIN CUCUMBER: a short, slim, rough-skinned cucumber. This variety is mainly used for pickling.

GINGER:
Fresh, green or root ginger: scrape away skin and grate, chop or slice as required.
Ground: should not be substituted for fresh ginger in any recipe.

GREEN SHALLOTS: also known as scallions, eschalots and green onions. Do not confuse with the small golden shallots.

GREEN TEA BAGS: also known as oolong tea.

HERBS: we have specified when to use fresh or dried herbs. Use dried (not ground) herbs in the proportions of 1:4 for fresh herbs, e.g. 1 teaspoon dried herbs instead of 4 teaspoons (1 tablespoon) chopped fresh herbs.

KATAIFI: packaged, shredded pastry bought chilled; it is available from delicatessens.

LAMB:
Minced: ground lamb.
Rack: row of cutlets.
Shank: forequarter leg.

LENTILS: dried pulses. There are many different varieties, usually identified and named after their colour.

MACADAMIAS: Queensland nuts or Hawaiian nuts.

MAPLE-FLAVOURED SYRUP: golden/pancake syrup; honey can be substituted.

MUSTARD:
Seeds: can be black or yellow.

OIL:
Extra virgin and virgin: the highest quality olive oils, obtained from the first pressings of the olives.
Light olive: mild-tasting, light in flavour, colour and aroma, but not low in kilojoules.
Olive: a blend of refined and virgin olive oils, especially good for everyday cooking.
Vegetable: we used a polyunsaturated vegetable oil.

Finger eggplant

Oregano

Thyme

Coriander

Basil

OKRA: a green, ridged, immature seed pod, also called lady's fingers.

ORANGE FLOWER WATER: concentrated flavouring made from orange blossoms.

PAPRIKA: ground dried peppers, available sweet or hot.

PEPPERS: capsicum or bell peppers.

PINE NUTS: small, cream-coloured soft kernels.

POMEGRANATE: round fruit, the size of a large orange, with thick, leathery red skin. Contains white seeds in pinkish-red, juicy, sweet pulp.

PUFF PASTRY SHEETS: frozen sheets of puff pastry made from wheat flour, vegetable margarine, salt, food acid and water.

QUINCE: yellow-skinned fruit with hard texture and acid taste.

RIND: zest.

ROCKET: a green salad leaf.

SAMBAL OELEK (also ulek or olek): a salty paste made from ground chillies.

SAUTERNES: a sweet, golden wine usually served with dessert.

SEMOLINA: a hard part of the wheat which is sifted out and used mainly for making pasta.

SESAME SEEDS: there are 2 types, black and white; we used white.
To toast: spread seeds evenly onto oven tray, toast in moderate oven for about 5 minutes or stir in heavy-based pan over heat until golden brown.

SPATCHCOCK: small chicken, weighing around 500g.

STAR ANISE: the dried star-shaped fruit of an evergreen tree, it has an aniseed flavour.

STOCK: 1 cup (250ml) stock is the equivalent of 1 cup (250ml) water plus 1 crumbled stock cube (or 1 teaspoon stock powder). If you prefer to make your own fresh stock, see recipes at right.

SUGAR: we used coarse granulated table sugar, also known as crystal sugar, unless otherwise specified.

Brown: a soft, fine granulated sugar containing molasses which gives it its characteristic colour.
Caster: also known as superfine; is fine granulated table sugar.
Icing sugar mixture: also known as confectioners' sugar or powdered sugar, with the addition of cornflour.
Pure icing sugar: also known as confectioners' sugar or powdered sugar.

SULTANAS: golden raisins.

SWEETENED CONDENSED MILK: we used canned milk from which 60% of the water had been removed; the remaining milk is then sweetened with sugar.

SWEET POTATO: fleshy white root vegetable.

TAGINE: a round dish with a conical lid; also the name of a recipe for meat or vegetable stew with fruit and nuts.

TAHINI PASTE: made from crushed sesame seeds.

TOMATO:
Canned: whole peeled tomatoes in natural juices.
Egg: also known as Roma, Italian or plum tomatoes.
Paste: a concentrated tomato puree used in flavouring soups, stews, sauces and casseroles, etc.
Puree: canned pureed tomatoes (not tomato paste). Use fresh, peeled, pureed tomatoes as a substitute, if preferred.

VANILLA BEAN: dried bean of the vanilla orchid. It can be used repeatedly, simply wash in warm water after use, dry well and store in airtight container.

VINEGAR:
Balsamic: originated in the province of Modena, Italy. Regional wine is specially processed then aged in antique wooden casks to give a pungent flavour.
Brown malt: made from fermented malt and beech shavings.
White: made from spirit of cane sugar.
White wine: is based on white wine.

VINE LEAVES: we used vine leaves in brine; available in jars and packets.

YEAST: allow 2 teaspoons (7g) dried yeast to each 15g compressed yeast if substituting one for the other.

ZA' ATAR SEASONING: dry blend of roasted sesame seeds, wild marjoram, thyme and sumac; available in Arabic specialty shops.

ZUCCHINI: courgette.

Make your own stock

These recipes can be made up to 4 days ahead and stored, covered, in the refrigerator. Be sure to remove any fat from the surface after the cooled stock has been refrigerated overnight. If the stock is to be kept longer, it is best to freeze it in smaller quantities. Stock is also available in cans or tetra packs. Be aware of their salt content. Stock cubes or powder can be used. As a guide, 1 teaspoon of stock powder or 1 small crumbled stock cube mixed with 1 cup (250ml) water will give a fairly strong stock. Be aware of the salt and fat content of stock cubes and powders.

BEEF STOCK
2kg meaty beef bones
2 medium (300g) onions
2 sticks celery, chopped
2 medium (250g) carrots, chopped
3 bay leaves
2 teaspoons black peppercorns
5 litres (20 cups) water
3 litres (12 cups) water, extra
Place bones and unpeeled chopped onions in baking dish. Bake in hot oven about 1 hour or until bones and onions are well browned. Transfer bones and onions to large pan, add celery, carrots, bay leaves, peppercorns and water, simmer, uncovered, 3 hours. Add extra water, simmer, uncovered, further 1 hour; strain.

FISH STOCK
1.5kg fish bones
3 litres (12 cups) water
1 medium (150g) onion, chopped
2 sticks celery, chopped
2 bay leaves
1 teaspoon black peppercorns
Combine all ingredients in large pan, simmer, uncovered, 20 minutes; strain.

CHICKEN STOCK
2kg chicken bones
2 medium (300g) onions, chopped
2 sticks celery, chopped
2 medium (250g) carrots, chopped
3 bay leaves
2 teaspoons black peppercorns
5 litres (20 cups) water
Combine all ingredients in large pan, simmer, uncovered, 2 hours; strain.

VEGETABLE STOCK
2 large (360g) carrots, chopped
2 large (360g) parsnips, chopped
4 medium (600g) onions, chopped
12 sticks celery, chopped
4 bay leaves
2 teaspoons black peppercorns
6 litres (24 cups) water
Combine all ingredients in large pan, simmer, uncovered, 1½ hours; strain.

All stock recipes make about 2.5 litres (10 cups).

Celeriac

Gherkin cucumber

Sweet potato

Eggplant

Index

QUICK CONVERSION GUIDE

Wherever you live in the world you can use our recipes with the help of our easy-to-follow conversions for all your cooking needs. These conversions are approximate only. The difference between the exact and approximate conversions of liquid and dry measures amounts to only a teaspoon or two, and will not make any difference to your cooking results.

MEASURING EQUIPMENT

The difference between measuring cups internationally is minimal within 2 or 3 teaspoons' difference. (For the record, 1 Australian metric measuring cup will hold approximately 250ml.) The most accurate way of measuring dry ingredients is to weigh them. When measuring liquids use a clear glass or plastic jug with metric markings.

If you would like the measuring cups and spoons as used in our Test Kitchen, turn to page 128 for details and order coupon. In this book we use metric measuring cups and spoons approved by Standards Australia.

- a graduated set of four cups for measuring dry ingredients; the sizes are marked on the cups.
- a graduated set of four spoons for measuring dry and liquid ingredients; the amounts are marked on the spoons.
- 1 TEASPOON: 5ml.
- 1 TABLESPOON: 20ml.

NOTE: NZ, CANADA, USA AND UK ALL USE 15ml TABLESPOONS.
ALL CUP AND SPOON MEASUREMENTS ARE LEVEL.

DRY MEASURES

METRIC	IMPERIAL
15g	½oz
30g	1oz
60g	2oz
90g	3oz
125g	4oz (¼lb)
155g	5oz
185g	6oz
220g	7oz
250g	8oz (½lb)
280g	9oz
315g	10oz
345g	11oz
375g	12oz (¾lb)
410g	13oz
440g	14oz
470g	15oz
500g	16oz (1lb)
750g	24oz (1½lb)
1kg	32oz (2lb)

LIQUID MEASURES

METRIC	IMPERIAL
30ml	1 fluid oz
60ml	2 fluid oz
100ml	3 fluid oz
125ml	4 fluid oz
150ml	5 fluid oz (¼ pint/1 gill)
190ml	6 fluid oz
250ml	8 fluid oz
300ml	10 fluid oz (½ pint)
500ml	16 fluid oz
600ml	20 fluid oz (1 pint)
1000ml (1 litre)	1¾ pints

WE USE LARGE EGGS WITH AN AVERAGE WEIGHT OF 60g

HELPFUL MEASURES

METRIC	IMPERIAL
3mm	⅛in
6mm	¼in
1cm	½in
2cm	¾in
2.5cm	1in
5cm	2in
6cm	2½in
8cm	3in
10cm	4in
13cm	5in
15cm	6in
18cm	7in
20cm	8in
23cm	9in
25cm	10in
28cm	11in
30cm	12in (1ft)

HOW TO MEASURE

When using the graduated metric measuring cups, it is important to shake the dry ingredients loosely into the required cup. Do not tap the cup on the bench, or pack the ingredients into the cup unless otherwise directed. Level top of cup with knife. When using graduated metric measuring spoons, level top of spoon with knife. When measuring liquids in the jug, place jug on flat surface, check for accuracy at eye level.

OVEN TEMPERATURES

These oven temperatures are only a guide; we've given you the lower degree of heat. Always check the manufacturer's manual.

	C° (Celsius)	F° (Fahrenheit)	Gas Mark
Very slow	120	250	1
Slow	150	300	2
Moderately slow	160	325	3
Moderate	180 – 190	350 – 375	4
Moderately hot	200 – 210	400 – 425	5
Hot	220 – 230	450 – 475	6
Very hot	240 – 250	500 – 525	7

TWO GREAT OFFERS FROM THE AWW HOME LIBRARY

Here's the perfect way to keep your Home Library books in order, clean and within easy reach. More than a dozen books fit into this smart silver grey vinyl folder. PRICE: Australia $11.95; elsewhere $21.95; prices include postage and handling. To order your holder, see the details below.

All recipes in the AWW Home Library are created using Australia's unique system of metric cups and spoons. While it is relatively easy for overseas readers to make any minor conversions required, it is easier still to own this durable set of Australian cups and spoons (photographed). PRICE : Australia: $5.95; New Zealand: $A8.00; elsewhere: $A9.95; prices include postage & handling.
his offer is available in all countries.

TO ORDER YOUR METRIC MEASURING SET OR BOOK HOLDER:

PHONE: Have your credit card details ready. Sydney: (02) 260 0035; **elsewhere in Australia:** 008 252 515 (free call, Mon-Fri, 9am-5pm) or FAX your order to (02) 267 4363 or MAIL your order by photocopying or cutting out and completing the coupon below.

PAYMENT: **Australian residents:** We accept the credit cards listed, money orders and cheques. **Overseas residents:** We accept the credit cards listed, drafts in $A drawn on an Australian bank, also English, New Zealand and U.S. cheques in the currency of the country of issue.
Credit card charges are at the exchange rate current at the time of payment.

Please photocopy and complete coupon and fax or send to:
AWW Home Library Reader Offer, ACP Direct, PO Box 7036, Sydney 2001.

❏ Metric Measuring Set   ❏ Holder

Please indicate number(s) required.

Mr/Mrs/Ms _____

Address_____

_____

Postcode _____ Country_____

Ph: ( ) _____Bus. Hour: _____

I enclose my cheque/money order for $ _____ payable to ACP Direct

OR: please charge my:

❏ Bankcard ❏ Visa ❏ MasterCard ❏ Diners Club ❏ Amex

☐☐☐☐☐☐☐☐☐☐☐☐☐☐☐☐ Exp. Date ___/__

Cardholder's signature _____

(Please allow up to 30 days for delivery within Australia. Allow up to 6 weeks for overseas deliveries.)

Both offers expire 30/6/96.   AWSF96